Dear Amber,

Happy 18th Birthday!

I can't believe we are this old and only getting older lol : ((

Love you lots and all our crazy mems, and hope to make many more!

Rebecca xxxxxx

# The Maddie Diaries

# The Maddie Diaries

## MADDIE ZIEGLER

SIMON &
SCHUSTER

London · New York · Sydney · Toronto · New Delhi

A CBS COMPANY

First published in Great Britain by Simon & Schuster UK Ltd, 2017
A CBS COMPANY

7 9 10 8 6

Simon & Schuster UK Ltd
1st Floor
222 Gray's Inn Road
London WC1X 8HB

www.simonandschuster.co.uk
www.simonandschuster.com.au
www.simonandschuster.co.in

Simon & Schuster Australia, Sydney
Simon & Schuster India, New Delhi

The author and publishers have made all reasonable efforts
to contact copyright-holders for permission, and apologise
for any omissions or errors in the form of credits given.
Corrections may be made to future printings.

A CIP catalogue record for this book
is available from the British Library.

ISBN: 978-1-4711-6496-5
Ebook ISBN: 978-1-4711-6497-2

Interior design by Jaime Putorti
Printed and bound by CPI Group (UK) Ltd, Croydon, CR0 4YY

MIX
Paper from
responsible sources
FSC® C020471

Simon & Schuster UK Ltd are committed to sourcing paper
that is made from wood grown in sustainable forests and support the Forest
Stewardship Council, the leading international forest certification organisation.
Our books displaying the FSC logo are printed on FSC certified paper.

# Contents

Introduction  *xi*

CHAPTER ONE

Presenting Madison Nicole  *1*

CHAPTER TWO

And Along Came Kenzie . . . *25*

CHAPTER THREE

Livin' on the Dance Floor  *43*

CHAPTER FOUR

It's Just Me  *81*

CHAPTER FIVE

Sia's Mini-Me  *107*

CHAPTER SIX

So I Think I Can Judge  *129*

CHAPTER SEVEN

Drama Queen  *143*

CHAPTER EIGHT

My Style File  *155*

CHAPTER NINE

## Makeup Maven  179

CHAPTER TEN

## The Me I've Yet to Meet  211

# *Foreword*

))⸻————————————————————((

*I* first laid eyes on Maddie during an episode of *Dance Moms*, which I had gotten sucked into somewhere along the way, and I remember seeing her and just thinking, *That face. That* face. There was something about her expressions that conveyed to me a real depth and wisdom and a feeling that I guess I could attune to. So when it came time to make a video for my song "Chandelier" I contacted [choreographer] Ryan Heffington and I said, I want to make this video with this little girl from this reality TV show. So I tweeted her and asked her if she would be in one of my videos, and we flew her out and she learned the entire dance in maybe an hour. The whole thing. It was absolutely incredible, and when my codirector Daniel [Askill] and I arrived on set to watch her map it out, we cried, we both cried because she's so special. So we did the video and we knew it was going to be important because we could all feel it on set. There was a great energy and everyone was completely amazed, the crew, everyone, they were just in awe, everyone was awed by this eleven-year-old and the punch that she packs. It became clear that she had a wisdom and maturity. She was so hypervigilant, reliable, responsible, a real combination of artist and pragmatist, which is something that I can relate to because I feel that way myself. So after that video I decided I never wanted to do anything without her. I felt a profound desire to protect her and to guide her through the entertainment industry because it was clear to me that she was going to be very successful and that it's very easy to be exploited, or to take the wrong path in this business.

So we talked about what she wanted, because it's a very overwhelming experience to become famous: In a sense, you lose your identity and you become what people believe you are, or they project onto you. I asked her what she loved doing the most and we ran down the list; she said she loved most of all dancing in front of people, and next she loved acting in films and videos, and after that it was modeling and TV shows. I believe that she's a channel, that she has an ability to get out of her own way and allow the source to come through her and speak through her. Whatever that source is I'm not sure, but it really does feel like she just has that. She's an artist. She can do it all. But at the same time, she's still just growing into this regular teenager, a kind, brilliant teenager. She doesn't whine, she's not rude, she's not snippy, she's not a mean girl. She is such a sweet person. Completely down-to-earth. And the more we traveled together the more I got to see that. On the plane or in the car she's always making goofy videos and has an excellent sense of humor, always playing pranks and just being herself. Her favorite food is sushi, her favorite fruit is blueberries, she really likes cake decorating and crafting, she's obsessed with makeup. She's really fun to be around. You can see that in how she is with her friends and with her fans. She's so nice to her fans and gives so much of herself.

At such a young age to have this profound of an impact on the world of dance, to have her contributions create a shift in commercial pop and the commercial dance landscape and to still be full of so much potential, it's inspiring. She inspires me not just to be a better artist but to be a better person. It makes me proud for the future, for people who feel strange and quirky and full of art but aren't sure how to express themselves, for young women everywhere. I can't wait to see where she takes it, to experience all the magic she lends to the universe.

*Sia*

*November 17, 2016*

# Introduction

))⊢————————————————⊣((

People think they know everything about me from *Dance Moms* or my Sia videos and I guess I understand how they might feel that way. I mean, I was completely hooked on *Gossip Girl*, and I felt like I knew all the characters on that show personally—we were family. I cried when I watched the last episode on Netflix because I truly felt like I was a part of their lives and I didn't want it to be over! Then I was shocked—I mean *shocked*—when I saw Ed Westwick (aka Chuck Bass) presenting at the People's Choice Awards and he started speaking with a British accent. I looked over at my mom: "What is going on? Why is he talking like Harry Potter?" I couldn't wrap my head around the fact that he was someone other than his character, a real person who just happened to be from England. Who knew? Then, as I listened to him, I realized I loved him *even more* when he was being truly himself. I've always thought British accents were cute . . .

So I get how people can make assumptions based on what they see or hear or read—it's easy to do that. Which is why I thought it was a really good idea to write a book. I may be only fourteen, but there are so many things I love and care about, and so many other sides of who I am. I want people to know the *real* me—the silly stuff, the serious stuff, and everything in between. I'm pretty sure you'll be surprised at some of what you learn. For example . . .

* I'm an artist: I love to draw faces—especially eyes—and paint. I just did a watercolor self-portrait. To be honest, it didn't really look like me, but I had fun trying. I did a painting for my room—it's black and white and kind of abstract, with a flower dripping down the middle. I also did one for Kenzie's room of lips and a nose, and I painted Olaf for my baby cousin. In fact, I drew all these doodles throughout the book!

* I cannot leave my house without spraying on my favorite perfume. I love the sweet vanilla scent, and I spray on *a lot*. I spray it inside my arms,

then on the back of my neck, and finally, I spray it in the air and walk through this cloud of perfume. My mom is always saying, "Maddie, you don't need that much!" but I insist. Maybe it's because the dance studios are always so stinky that I feel the need to smell good!

* I don't wear my hair in a perfect bun all the time. In reality, a messy topknot is my go-to style when I'm not onstage. It's the easiest thing to do. I just scoop it and clip it up, without even looking in the mirror!

* When I was three or four years old, I broke my arm just when I was supposed to start horseback riding, so I couldn't. Looking back, I'm really glad that happened—even though at the time I remember being upset. I might have been a horseback rider instead of a dancer! Things definitely happen for a reason, and I believe in fate.

* I have a wish list in my head of things I want to do, see, and be. And I believe in making wishes. Whenever my friends and I see the time 11:11 on a clock,

we touch something blue and make a wish. I don't really know why, but it seemed like a good idea and it kinda stuck . . . it's like a superstition now.

* Dancing didn't come naturally to me—I wasn't very good at it in the beginning, and I had to work really hard. It taught me an important lesson: Even if you're not good at something at first, don't give up. Someday you will look back and never believe how far you've come.

* I believe in taking time-outs every now and then. People think I am in the dance studio 24/7, every second of the day. I do dance every day, but I also have a home and friends that I hang with (more on that later). My family recently went to Aruba on vacation and I loved every minute of it (except for the sunburn—I looked like a lobster!). Sia taught me this: If you don't want to be doing what you're doing, if you're feeling overwhelmed or stressed and the passion isn't there, then it's okay to walk away for a little while. You're allowed to take a second to breathe; you don't have to keep going and going.

✳ I'm okay with being a loser. In the beginning of my competitive dancing, I always wanted to win and I'd get mad or upset if I didn't. But now I know that losing is good. It makes you work harder the next time and learn and grow from your mistakes. It makes you a better performer and a better person.

✳ Our dog Maliboo is a diva. Every night she has to go out at 4 a.m. to pee and my stepdad has to get up, go downstairs, and open the door for her. Technically, she's Mackenzie's dog, but there's no way my little sister is losing any beauty sleep . . .

✳ I have a bedtime routine: I put a barrier of pillows around me so I feel comfy and protected, and I can only fall asleep if I watch TV before I go to bed. Right now, I'm binge-watching *Grey's Anatomy*.

✳ I have an amazing memory. Seriously, I don't forget anything—I remember things from when I was a toddler. I never kept a journal when I was little, because I didn't feel the need to write stuff down. But I can tell you every detail of what happened when I was younger and how I felt at that time—it's like hitting rewind, and it really comes in handy when you're writing a book!

And those are just a few things off the top of my head. My mom has also kept every picture of me over the years (even the embarrassing ones) in boxes, and a ton of those are in here, too. But I have a whole other reason for writing this book—one that doesn't involve me at all. It's about *you*. I want to encourage you to believe in yourself and follow your passion. Everyone has a talent and a gift; everyone can make an impact. I know I'm just a teenager, but if you haven't noticed, teens are changing the world. More than ever, we have a voice through social media and a way to connect, educate, and make a difference. We are the future, and girls especially are awesome. There is nothing that we can't do if we put our minds to it. See the possibilities and don't let stuff or people hold you back.

I always thought I would be "just a competitive dancer." But now, I realize that was only the beginning. I'm just figuring out what makes me happy and excited and pushing myself to try new things and stretch my wings. I guess my philosophy is "Why not?" Why not do something that you've never done before? Why not dream big? Why not stand up for things you believe in? Sometimes you have to take a big, scary leap, and that's okay. Even if you fall on your butt, you've still soared.

*Madison*

· Chapter One ·

# PRESENTING
# MADISON NICOLE

y mom likes the letter *M*. Seriously—that's why she named me Madison and my sister Mackenzie, because she likes the letter. I'm glad she didn't like the letter *X*, because I can't think of a single girl's name that starts with it! My middle name, Nicole, was after her niece. She also liked being pregnant (I can't really understand that one!) and she had a really big belly when she was carrying me around. I was huge when I was born—9 pounds, 10 ounces; 21.5 inches—and kind of stubborn. I refused to come out for forty-two weeks, and no matter what the doctors and the hospital tried, I wouldn't exit on my own. So my mom had a C-section, and then I made my grand entrance.

My mom will tell you that I was the easiest baby. Happy, quiet, and a really good sleeper who was very considerate and didn't wake my parents up in the middle of the night (you're welcome!). When I was six months old, my mom could literally go get a mani and a pedi or get her hair colored with me right there beside her. I didn't make a peep; I never cried or fussed. Most of the time I just napped. And when I got old enough to eat, I would eat anything and everything. I was never picky and always adventurous—which I still am. If you put alligator in front of me and dare me to take a bite, I will. My first word was *Mama*, and when I stood up at ten months old, my mom actually tried to knock me down. She knew that once I walked I would start running and there would be no stopping me!

A lot of parents have trouble potty-training their kids. Again, mine really lucked out. My sister Mackenzie was just born, so I was a little more than a year and a half old. One day, I proudly brought my little plastic portable potty outside in the yard to where my mom was pushing Kenzie in her swing. I announced, "No more diapies," and marched right back in the house. That was that. Once I made my mind up, there was no telling me anything else. And especially with a little baby sister, I wanted to be "the big girl" in the house. Mackenzie didn't know it, but she kind of had two mommies—me and my mom. I taught her everything I knew, including her ABCs and some math, like 1 + 1 and 2 + 2, when she was way too little to read or count. She could count to twenty when she was only sixteen months old thanks to me! When she came along, I was excited: Now I had someone to play with all the time. My mom would always put us in matching outfits and so many people would ask if we were twins. When I was four, I finally stood up for myself: "Mom, no more matching! Pullease!" So instead, she would coordinate us; the looks weren't *exactly* the same, but they went well together.

As a toddler, I was always on the move. I started dancing when I was two years old at Laurel Ballet in Greensburg, Pennsylvania. I remember loving *The Wiggles* and *Hi-5* on TV. I would jump up and down and sing, "Five, four, three, two, one, come with us and have some fun!" whenever they were on TV. Hi-5 were like a pop band for little kids, and I knew every song and the choreography by heart. My mom says I begged to see them in concert, but so did every other kid on the planet and they sold out in seconds. So she went on eBay and got me tickets (now *that's* a great mom!). I was also really into *Bear in the Big Blue House* on Playhouse Disney. We saw him one summer at Disney World, and my mom and I burst into tears because I loved him so, so much. When I got a little older, I watched the Disney Channel all the time: *Hannah Montana, Wizards of Waverly Place, The Suite Life of Zack & Cody, High School Musical.* That's when I started to be obsessed with Zac Efron—and I still am. Sia knows this and once called me right before I was supposed to come over to her house.

"Do you want to meet Zac Efron?" she asked.

My heart started pounding. "Um, yeah. Why?"

"Would you be cool or would you be starstruck?" she pressed on.

I had to be honest. "I would try to keep my cool, but I'd probably have a panic attack or faint. Why?"

"I want to make that happen," she said. So of course, I went to her house thinking I was going to walk in and see Troy Bolton sitting there on her living room couch. No such luck, but I don't think she was just teasing. I'm convinced she is going to make it happen one day, when I least expect it. Sia likes surprises.

But it's no secret: I think everyone who knows me knows Zac is my ultimate guy. I was once on this road trip with Mackenzie, Kendall Vertes, and our moms, and we kids were sitting in the backseat totally bored. I decided to check out what new movies were on Netflix, and there it was: *Charlie St. Cloud*, Zac's first big dramatic film. We started watching it and were only halfway through when we reached our hotel.

"Girls, it's late," my mom said. "No more movies."

I begged. I pleaded. How could I just end it right smack in the middle? Finally, my mom was so tired, she just gave in. "Fine, but go right to sleep after it's over."

So I sat there in the dark in bed with my headphones on while everyone else was sleeping. I continued watching the movie and sobbing my eyes out because it's the saddest thing I have ever seen. Ever.

It was close to midnight when my mom woke up. She looked worried. "Maddie, are you okay?" she asked. I was literally bawling.

"It's just so, so sad," I cried. "His little brother is dead and they're playing ball!"

My mom was totally confused. And of course, I was so upset over the movie, I couldn't sleep that night. It was *that* real. So if I ever meet Zac in person, I can't promise I won't totally freak. I still think of that movie and get teary-eyed.

I'm very sentimental over all things *High School Musical*. I watched all three of the movies on the Disney Channel when they recently had a marathon in honor of the movie's tenth anniversary. Zac's a good guy. I saw that he surprised Olympic gold medalist Simone Biles and her gymnastics team on the *Today* show because she had a huge crush on him. I was so, so jealous. She had pics of him all over her Instagram and he *kissed* her. I would *die*.

The other day I was in the pool swimming and I pulled out this *High School Musical* towel to dry myself off. It was so tiny, it barely covered my knees, but I remember it being huge when I was small and how much I loved draping it around me. Ten years ago I was about four when the movie was out. It seems like yesterday. I had all the sound tracks and DVDs, and when my friends would come over for play-dates, we'd act out the scenes or get out my *High School Musical* dolls. I remember the Corbin Bleu one in his green T-shirt and Sharpay with her "Bop to the Top" blue dress. They were like mini Barbies, just a little smaller than a regular doll, and some played music so they "sang" when you pressed a button on their back. My favorite scene in *High School Musical 2* is the end, where Miley Cyrus has this two-second cameo in the finale, the beach party scene. We would try to freeze the DVD right at the second she's on-screen.

When my grandparents came over, Mackenzie and I would put on a show for them in the kitchen. She would pretend to be Sharpay, and we'd bring in a beach chair, sunglasses, and a bag, and she'd come out in her bathing suit, reciting all the lines from *High School Musical 2* by heart. She loved being the mean girl! Or we'd take turns playing Gabriella and Troy and acting out their scenes and duets: "We're soaring! Flyin'!" Actually, Kenzie always wanted to be Gabriella, because she was smaller, but I never liked playing a boy. So we'd fight over it and my mom would have to step in and referee. Of course, Kenzie would still get her way, and I had to put my hair up so I looked like a boy.

I hear they're making *High School Musical 4* with all new characters, and I have to say I'm not so sure how that will work. Don't get me wrong, I'll definitely watch it. But it's not the characters that I loved and connected to. Without them, it won't be the same. I think about how my cousin is five now, and she will watch it and maybe get as attached to it as I got to the movie ten years ago. We really rooted for them: for the Wildcats to win; for Gabriella and Troy to find love even though he was a jock and she was a brain; for Sharpay to stop being so mean; and for Ryan to finally have his chance in the spotlight. When I think back on my childhood, it has this special place, and I know a lot of teens who feel that way about it. We all wanted to be them because they had so much fun and things turned out fine in the end because they were a team and worked together.

Another big part of my childhood was collecting stuff. When I say "stuff," I mean lots of little things with even smaller pieces that we were always losing and my mom was always stepping on. Like a Polly Pocket shoe. I had piles of Pollys and dozens and dozens of Littlest Pet Shop animals. I was also really into those little "squishies" you get in the vending machine at the supermarket. They were these little rubber figures shaped like fruit and animals with a hole in one end so you could use them as a pencil topper. I kept them in this little wallet, and I would brag to my friends when I got the rare ones. Every time we'd go to the grocery store, I'd beg for more. We were also big on dolls. Mackenzie had every set of the Bitty Twins: the blondes, the brunettes, the African American ones. I was more into the American Girl dolls, because I loved their long hair that you could style. We had thirteen in total, which I know is crazy! But I wanted the latest historical one every Christmas or birthday. We'd play house, pretending we were both married (me to Zac Efron, and Kenzie to Justin Bieber), and all the dolls would be our kids. I'd pretend to be on the phone with my husband: "Hi, honey! How's your day?" We had this toy salon chair, and I would be the stylist, and the American Girls were all my clients. Each one would get a new look: braids, buns, pigtails, ponytails, updo, half-updo, even a French twist. I learned how to do my own hair for shows and competitions by practicing on them. Kenzie's favorite American Girl was Kit—the one from the Great Depression. She has short blond hair (which always made it tough for me to style). I'd have to say my favorite was a look-alike doll I named Chloe. I know the idea is you're supposed to choose a doll that looks just like you, but instead, I went for one with long blond hair. Way more fun in my opinion. I also loved Molly because she came with glasses. Of course, we lost them almost immediately . . .

We had this craft drawer in our laundry room filled with colored paper, stickers, paints, markers, crayons, glitter glue. If it was a rainy day, or I was ever bored or looking for something to do, I just opened it up and created some project out of my imagination. We painted a lot of canvases, but I think our favorite thing to make was thank-you notes and cards for people. We never had to go buy one at the Hallmark store. We also had these coloring books with faces, where you could use crayons or colored pencils to do their "makeup." I could spend hours on this, creating dramatic smoky eyes and red lips for my girls and dreaming of where they would be going all made up. Maybe on a date . . . or to the prom . . . or some red-carpet movie premiere.

My favorite thing to do in elementary school was go to the playground and hang from the monkey bars. I would have calluses on my hands from doing my tricks and hanging there, upside down. I was pretty fearless. When I got a little older, I volunteered in one of my teachers' kindergarten classes. I would come in thirty minutes early and help her set up; then I would work with her students, going over their letters with them or putting stars on their papers. I guess I've always loved working with little kids—there's something about their energy and the way they are so excited to learn and experience new things. The world is such a big, cool place to them, and it's fun to see things through their eyes. Sometimes I think I'd make a pretty good teacher.

My family always took a yearly trip to Disney World, and we have tons of photos of me and my sister with every princess you can think of. My two favorites are Ariel and Cinderella, so I'd always get in line for them, even if it was a mile long. I was patient; Kenzie not so much. I had this book that we filled with their autographs. Sometimes Kenzie would get up there after waiting an hour or more and burst into tears; the characters scared her when she was really small. She was probably thinking, *Who is the strange lady wearing seashells?* Or, *Why is there this big mouse with a giant head hugging me?* It cracked me up. We loved running through the sprinklers and going on all the rides. Now that we're older and spend a lot more time in L.A., we go to Disneyland instead. It's great, but not quite the same: The castle isn't as big, and some of the rides are different. I think my favorite part of the park is the California Adventure side. When I was little, I used to be terrified of roller coasters—you couldn't bribe me to go on one. But now I can't get enough of them. California Screamin' has about five thousand flips (not kidding!), and it's the perfect name for it because you scream your head off the entire ride. I guess what I love is the adrenaline rush, how the coaster climbs, climbs, climbs to the top, then drops down and takes your breath away. My mom won't go on them; she says they make her sick. But I love any thrill ride. One time, when we were visiting Australia for *Dance Moms*, we went on the Superman roller coaster at Warner Bros. Movie World. It literally speeds up from zero to a hundred kilometers per hour in two seconds; it's one of the fastest coasters in the world and you feel like your head is going to explode! Because we were there for a press tour, we had security guards who were able to get us to the front of the line without waiting. I rode it four times in a row—not even a break in between. One of my dance teachers who was with us quit after two times and said she was going to throw up if she did it again. But me? I kept on going.

People have always told me that I'm "an old soul." When I was younger, I wasn't sure what that meant, or if it was a particularly nice thing to be—it sounded like an insult. But now, I understand it and I agree. I've always been mature and responsible; I've always acted older than I am. Perfect example: I hate to be late for anything, and when you're in L.A., being on time is nearly impossible. The traffic is crazy, bumper-to-bumper in all four lanes on the freeway, and you just sit there, stuck. When I have an audition or a show to get to, I sit down with my mom and make a plan how to get there and how long it will take. Then I add on like an hour! The other day we were going to an audition that was nine miles away and I swear it took us an hour and a half! Most kids don't worry about this, I know. But you can set a watch by me. I'm just someone who likes to be punctual and on a good day, early. I think it shows that you're on top of things and you care. I'm super organized—I will always lay out my outfit the night before. And I don't believe in wasting money, which is the opposite of how Mackenzie feels. I always tell my mom, "It's okay, you don't have to buy it for me, I don't need it," while my sister has a long, long list of stuff she wants/needs/has to have. I'm more practical—I save for a rainy day. I don't think you need an expensive bag because it has a fancy label. Kenzie, however, would do just about *anything* for a Louis Vuitton bag. Maybe even her chores, for once!

I've also always been someone who thinks and analyzes and tries to consider what it's like to be in someone else's shoes. I feel really deeply about things; I take them to heart. If something makes me mad or sad, I can't just sit there and not do anything about it. I want to fix things. I don't like to see or hear that something is unfair or unjust, that people are suffering, especially kids. My mom always visited nursing homes when I was little. She loved talking to older people, and I'm the same way. Most of my friends today are a lot older than me. I've always been really comfortable around grown-ups, and they're comfortable around me because I don't think or act like I'm a kid. If I was quiet when I was little, it's most likely because I was thinking—not because I was shy or afraid.

Looking back on my little-kid days, I think I'm still the same person—just in a bigger body. I just had a growth spurt and now I'm taller than my mom, which is funny—she has to look up to me when she's telling me what to do! My personality has stayed the same: I still act goofy when I'm with my friends and family, and I try and crack silly jokes or make them laugh. My American Girl dolls may be tucked away in the closet now, but I still love to do hair (usually mine, my friends' or Mackenzie's) in crazy dos. My room definitely looks different—I've gone from pink and purple to gray, black, and white. I think it's more grown-up, less Disney princess, and I really love to decorate. I could seriously have a career as an interior decorator. Just the other day I was in Crate and Barrel and found this fluffy pillow I couldn't resist. I love to look through decorating magazines for ideas or watch those extreme makeover shows on TV—how cool would it be to redo an entire *house*? But the furniture in my bedroom is still the same—I have my dresser and bed that I had when I was seven years old. I love new stuff, but I'm also sentimental. I like things that remind me of who I was, things that feel safe and familiar.

The thing that has changed the most is how I think. I do a lot of "big picture" thinking now, not just living in the moment or letting other people around me make the decisions. I have a voice and an opinion. I think about the person I want to be and what I can do to get myself there. I think about being a role model and the impact my words and actions can have on others. My mom always tells me that I've been given this gift—kids look up to me and listen to what I say. If they're listening and watching, then I want to empower them to do great things with their lives! Like I used to teach Kenzie her ABCs, I'd like to teach kids to stop bullying each other, to respect that everyone is unique and special in their own way, and make them understand that we all have so much to give and share with each other.

I used to worry a lot about what people thought or said about me, and now I've come to realize you need to own who you are. You can't let others dictate that for you. You can't mold yourself to fit someone else's image or expectations. My confidence has soared in so many ways. I used to worry about what I was wearing and spend hours rummaging through my closet: Would my friends like it? Was it cool or trendy enough? Now I wear what makes me feel good, what I like because it makes me smile or walk a little taller and hold my head up high. I also think I've learned to relax more. I don't just mean hanging out at the pool with friends. I mean I've relaxed my attitude. Even as an eight-year-old, I took things so seriously and I was nervous all the time. I was *intense.* Today, I laugh more. I don't feel like everything is riding on getting one acting gig or winning one dance performance. You can't stress about everything all the time.

I know there's a lot of pressure on teens—we're stuck in between being kids and being adults and we want to be taken seriously. But you don't have to be perfect. I know that now: It's okay to have a bad-hair day. It's okay to mess up on a test or lose a soccer game. It happens. Honestly, it happens to me a lot. I try really hard not to judge myself so harshly the way I used to. I tell myself, "There's always tomorrow, you can always do better." And I really love the idea that the future is filled with so many possibilities—what will I try next? What's out there that I haven't even discovered yet? I give myself a few minutes to be angry or disappointed; then I move on—no dwelling. I like to be someone always moving forward. I guess that hasn't changed much since I was a toddler—no one could hold me back then, and I like to think no one can hold me back now.

# Shhh! Don't Tell ...

## STUFF NOBODY KNOWS ABOUT ME (AND NOW YOU DO!)

* **I love Nicholas Sparks movies.** *The Best of Me*, *The Longest Ride*, and *The Choice* are my all-time faves. I love how they're sad, romantic, and dramatic all rolled up into one. I have to watch them with a box of Kleenex.

* **I can rap.** Pretty much any Drake song, I know all the words.

* **The character I am most like on *Gossip Girl* is Serena.** She always has really cute outfits and she's a very caring friend.

* **The character I *wish* I could be more like on *Grey's Anatomy* is Izzie.** She literally gets emotionally invested in every patient. She has the biggest heart. She's also really fun—and bold. She says what's on her mind.

* **At Dairy Queen, I will always order . . .** a chocolate-chip Blizzard with chocolate sprinkles mixed into it. Yum!

* **I make silly videos for Sia.** Usually makeup tutorials. The other day I pretended to be Miranda Sings putting on eyeliner.

* **I met supermodel Gigi Hadid at the Tommy Hilfiger show** and she is super sweet. I love her style, I love her hair. Basically, I'd love to *be* her—at least for one day.

* **When I was seven, I had my own YouTube channel** where I did face painting. I could make myself look like a vampire, an Avatar . . .

* **I'd love to be a member of Fifth Harmony.** Seriously, they could just rename the group Sixth Harmony, and it would be cool with me. Just one prob: I can't sing. So maybe I could just be their backup dancer? I love their music and I love what they stand for: girl power!

* **People think I'm crazy confident, but I'm really insecure about my skin.** I hate zits. If I have one, I'm like, "I can't go out with this thing in the middle of my forehead!" Luckily, I'm really good at concealing with makeup. Cover-up is a girl's best friend. I also used to hate my teeth—I think they're too big, and people used to write some mean comments about them on my social media. But Tonya Brewer, my hair and makeup

stylist, thinks they're cute, and has taught me to love them. When we were backstage waiting to go on at *SNL*, I drew a picture of them on her. The next thing I knew, she had my doodle added to her arm as a permanent tattoo! She wanted to prove to me that I'm beautiful exactly as I am, and I should never change.

* **If I could dye my hair any color and not have my mom freak out,** it would be blond. I mean, she colors her hair. Sorry, Mom, I think that was *your* secret!

* **My favorite thing to shop for is shoes.** The Nordstrom shoe department in L.A. is my happy place. My everyday shoes are Adidas sneakers because they're comfy. But otherwise, I'm crazy for Jimmy Choo, Dior, Valentino, YSL . . . they're like walking works of art. Honestly, I would love to have a shoe museum in my closet so I could display them.

* **I could eat an entire bag of . . .** goldfish crackers. The cheesy ones. You know the ones little kids like to eat? The other day I was home in my apartment in L.A. and I was starving. All I could find was goldfish. So I ate handful after handful until there were just crumbs left. Kenzie's gonna be so mad.

## Dear Maddie

### YOU ASKED...I ANSWERED!

**I'm thirteen, and I look at all the girls in my dance studio and think they are so much skinnier than me! I feel like a blob! I'm always comparing my body to theirs.**

Okay, I have my blob days, too, when I feel like everyone is skinnier or prettier than me. It's called being a teenager. I promise you, every girl in your studio has probably felt the way you do at one time or another. When you hit puberty, your body kind of goes crazy. Cut yourself a little slack as you go through these changes. Beyond that, if you're eating healthy and dancing regularly, you shouldn't have to worry about being skinny. Skinny doesn't necessarily mean healthy or pretty, and it's not a smart goal to have for yourself. Instead, try to practice good habits: Drink lots of water, make sure to get enough protein and veggies, and don't overdo the junk food. I do my best. Just the other day I had quinoa for the first time and it was life-changing! Try not to be so critical of yourself. Love yourself for who you are, inside and out.

THE Maddie DIARIES

**My ballet teacher is always picking on me and pointing out when I do something wrong. Why does she hate me?**

I don't think your teacher hates you. The teacher who picks on you the most usually also cares about you the most—he or she sees the potential and wants you to improve. I know it's hard to listen to someone saying negative things about you, but correction and constructive criticism is part of being a dancer. Don't take it personally. I know, I know, easier said than done. But remind yourself that your teacher just wants you to be the best dancer you can be.

**There's this boy in my school I am crushing on but he doesn't know I'm alive. I don't know if I should say anything to him—what if it scares him away?**

Okay, do not, I repeat, *do not* go up to him and say, "I have a major crush on you." He'll think you're weird and probably run away. Who could blame him? That's a lot to take in all at once. Instead, start up a casual conversation—maybe about a class or a hobby you have in common. Be friends first, then build from there. He'll get to know you better and you can figure out if the feeling is mutual.

## Today Is a Beautiful Day to . . .

One of my favorite sayings on *Grey's Anatomy* is "It's a beautiful day to save lives." The characters say it to each other, and Kalani Hilliker, JoJo Siwa, and my other *Grey's*-loving friends and I have kind of picked up on it. But it also got me thinking—what is today a beautiful day to do? I consider that question and make a little mental list, then make sure to check it off. I think it helps you feel more energetic and optimistic if you have a reason to do something fun, helpful, or healthy with your time. You can come up with your own list (the more creative the better), but I thought I'd give you a few in every chapter to get you going!

* Text a friend that you miss her/him. It can really make someone's day to know you're thinking about them (include a smiley-face emoji). I know it makes mine.

* Try a new food, something you've never tasted before. I ordered this curry apple chicken salad today from Lemonade, a California cuisine restaurant that does takeout, and it was surprisingly yum.

* Act like a little kid. Kenzie and I just went to Disneyland for the day and spun around on the teacup ride

until we were dizzy. It reminded us how much we used to love the park when we were little. I also went to the American Girl doll store to pick out some stuff for my little cousin. I really missed that place, especially the salon where they pierce the dolls' ears. The point is, find something you used to love to do when you were younger and do it—read your favorite Dr. Seuss book, break out the crayons and coloring book, watch the Disney Channel (incidentally, I just found *Hannah Montana* On Demand on my TV the other day and watched for two hours straight!). Doing any of the above makes me feel really sentimental and happy.

• *Chapter Two* •

# AND ALONG CAME KENZIE...

I was only a year old when my mom broke the news to me that I was going to be "a big sissy." I'm sure I had no idea what that meant at the time, but nine months later, when Mackenzie was born, I got it: She was part of our family, and I loved her with all my heart. I kissed her and kissed her and kissed her. I would squeeze her so tight that she would turn bright red in the face—she looked like a tomato. My parents would have to pry her out of my arms. To me, she was a little doll, a toy to be cuddled and played with. I didn't understand that she was actually *real* and I had to be gentle because she was so tiny and fragile. As she got a little older and learned to talk, she never stopped. And I mean, *never*—Mackenzie is always talking, singing, bossing me around. She has a knack for interrupting whenever I'm talking, and if I'm telling a story, she has to correct it: "Nuh-uh, that's not how it happened . . ." Whenever my dance friends come over for sleepovers, she tries to wriggle her way into the party—which makes me furious. They're my friends, and I want to spend private time with them.

"Can't you go hang out with *your* friends?" I ask her.

But what's mine is hers—that's what she thinks, anyway. Even if she doesn't like what we're doing, she still wants to be a part of it. My neighbors and I recently decided we would go see the horror movie *The Conjuring 2* and Kenzie insisted she wanted to come along.

"You'll hate it," I told her. "You'll be terrified and cry."

"Will not!" she told me. "I'm not a baby."

So off we all went to the movie theater, my sister trailing along. The previews for some upcoming horror movies started and she was already hiding her eyes and climbing in our laps. Fifteen minutes into the movie—before anything creepy had actually happened—she was under her seat, petrified. She crawled out and started walking—actually running—from the auditorium.

"Wait!" I called after her. "Where are you going?"

"Home!" she said. It turns out she had texted my mom and stepdad to come pick her up in the theater parking lot. She couldn't stand the movie for one more minute. I hate to say it, but told ya so!

Mackenzie gets to do a lot more than I was allowed to do at her age—she has much more independence, and I think that's because I broke my mom in for her. I'm a teenager and she's still twelve, but she still gets to do practically everything I do. She's always gotten away with a lot more than I have. Part of it is her being the baby of the family; part of it is her being so good at manipulating people and situations. It's a talent, and as much as it annoys me, I've grown to accept it— or at least marvel at Mackenzie in action.

I remember when we were little, she'd hit me really hard for no apparent reason then race downstairs and find my mom before I could tell on her.

"Mommy!" she'd cry, "Maddie hit me!"

Total lie, but she was incredibly convincing, an Oscar-winning actress. I got yelled at every time for beating up my little sister when she was the one hitting me! My mom is probably reading this right now and saying, "Oh my gosh! I never knew that!" That's how good she was at fibbing.

The kid is a troublemaker. Go ahead and ask her and she will admit it. She's actually *proud* of the fact. She is always the one saying, "Hey, I've got an idea . . ." and I'm the one warning her, "No, we're gonna get in trouble." I'm the voice of reason and she's the voice of crazy. Like when she wants to play Ding Dong Ditch (when you knock on a door and run away) when we're staying in a hotel. I say no, she says yes, and somehow, even though I was trying to talk her out of it, I get caught and scolded. You would think I would have learned after all these years, but no! Kenzie gets me every time. She's also always flipping around. She literally cannot stand still without doing a cartwheel, a backflip, a somersault, an aerial. I think she's happiest upside down.

That's kind of our relationship: She's the fun one, and I'm the serious one. People ask if we fight. We're sisters; of course we fight. We fight all the time. But we also forget what the fight is about five minutes later. That's the way it goes, and I know it drives my mom and my stepdad, Greg, up the walls to hear us bickering, but most of the time it's over silly stuff like who said what, or who did what. Kenzie always wants my opinion on things. My mom says I should be flattered, but I'm worried that when she's grown up, she'll be driving on a road and call me up: "Maddie, do I go right or left? What do you think I should do?" I want her to learn to stand on her own two feet, and to have her own opinions, likes, and dislikes. I don't need her to take mine! A lot of our arguments have to do with the fact that she expects me to share everything with her—my clothes, my makeup, even my food—and she doesn't like to share any of her things with me. It's a double standard. She likes me to do everything for her—like she's still the baby—and gets really impatient if I say, "Can you just wait a sec?" For example, this morning I was in the middle of eating my breakfast, racing to get to a warm-up class I was leading, and she comes into the kitchen and demands I do her hair for her. I literally had to drop everything I was doing "or else." I'm not sure what the "or else" was—probably that she would go run and tell my mom or Greg that I was being mean to her—but I did it. Sometimes it's just easier to let her have her way—there's less whining involved. When my mom hears us arguing, she'll tell us to stop, and we always say, "We're not fighting," even if we are. So I don't think she knows half of what really goes on between us. If she did, we'd both be grounded for at least a year!

I have to be careful sharing any secrets with Mackenzie. She'll keep them, but then one day she'll hold it over my head and threaten to tell—unless I give her something she wants, like a shirt in my closet. I always wonder how she gets away with *everything*, even things that make no sense. One day she called me from Pittsburgh when I was in New York working.

"Maddie, guess what? I got a pet chicken." My jaw literally hit the floor.

"You *what*?" I knew she and her friend had been talking for a while about how much they loved little baby chicks, but I didn't think she'd go through with it. It's not like we have a farm in our backyard! The song is "Old MacDonald," ee-i-ee-i-o, not "Old Mackenzie"!

"You did not. Stop lying."

"Did, too," Mackenzie insisted. "You can hear them!" She held the phone up and I heard "Cheep! Cheep!" in the background. She wasn't kidding. This is what happens when I go off to film for a few weeks?

"Mom is gonna freak," I told her. "Does she know?"

"They're in a pen in my friend's living room," she assured me.

"*They*? There's more than one?"

"Well, the farm said we had to take six . . . and they're all so cute and little and fuzzy!"

This went on for about two weeks, with Mackenzie convinced she was going to teach them to lay eggs and we'd have fresh omelets every day for breakfast. The chicks started growing into chickens, and Kenzie's friend's dad had to build a bigger pen outside. Eventually, they gave two of the six away so they'd have enough room—and they wouldn't eat both families out of house and home. So now we had four chickens cooped up in her friend's backyard, getting bigger by the day. Kenzie loved and fed them and took care of them, until we made a shocking discovery: Three of the four were male roosters, not female chickens.

"You mean they can't lay eggs?" Kenzie asked, pouting. Major disappointment. Eventually, all the chickens/roosters went to live on a farm, where they were much happier. I couldn't say the same, though, for my sister. In her mind, this was an epic fail. I tried to convince her that *normal* people don't keep pet chickens in the house, but she will never admit she was wrong. Ever.

If I want to annoy Kenzie it's pretty simple: I hug her. She hates when I squeeze her super tight in a bear hug and she gets all squirmy. But just recently, I've noticed our relationship has started to change. We were on a FaceTime call the other day (FYI, we never FaceTime, so that alone was a rarity), and she was home in Pittsburgh, and I was out in L.A. shooting *So You Think You Can Dance: The Next Generation*. We talked for a really long time, without fighting even once. We talked like friends, not sisters. When she finally came out to L.A., we were so happy to see each other, I even got a long hug without her trying to wriggle away. They say absence makes the heart grow fonder. I guess that's true, because we really, truly missed each other and were so glad to be back together. But I also think we're growing up and we realize that some things are worth fighting about and others aren't. Do I like when Mackenzie "borrows," aka takes, and doesn't return my favorite mascara without asking my permission? No. But is it worth not speaking to my sister over? Not really. It's just a thing, and people are more important than things. Family is most important of all.

When we were younger, I would protect Mackenzie, holding her hand and making sure she didn't trip or fall or bump into any walls when she was learning how to walk. I would spot her on the monkey bars until she got so good on them, she didn't need my help. If she was scared or sad or crying, I would put my arms around her, rest her head on my shoulder, and tell her it would be okay. Today, I feel like she's fiercely protective of me. If someone makes a nasty comment aimed at me, she is the first to race to my side to defend me. I remember one time, a girl in school was being mean and hurting my feelings. I felt bullied, and without telling me, Kenzie took my phone and texted her, "She didn't do anything, cut it out." At first, I wasn't thrilled that she a) stole my phone and b) sent a text behind my back. But then I thought about it: That was pretty brave of her to stand up to that girl. It took a lot of courage and a lot of caring. Though she would never admit it, I know Kenzie would do anything for me. She's not one to get all mushy and say she loves me, but her actions speak louder than words.

My mom got us these gold Jennifer Meyer necklaces for Christmas that say SISTER. We never take them off. Though she drives me nuts, there's a lot I admire about my little sister, and a lot I can learn from her. She's a free spirit, and she always sees the humor in every situation—even the ones that are frustrating or confusing. She's always optimistic, and if someone isn't having a good time, she knows how to make one happen. She has a hard time taking no for an answer (especially when I'm the one saying no), and I actually think that's an amazing quality to have. She sees what's possible, even if it's not in front of her face. She's hilarious—she makes me laugh so hard my sides hurt. I can't imagine what my life would be like without her in it. I can't imagine going through everything I've been through these past several years without her there on the journey with me—even if she bugged me sometimes (okay, a lot of the time!). She looks up to me, and because she does, it makes me want to set a good example for how to act, treat others, and live my life. We push each other to be better people all around, which I think is what sisters should do.

Like it or not, Kenz, you're getting a hug when I finish writing this.

*I know it's my book,
but I had to give my little sister
a chance to say something . . .*

## *Kenzie:* A FEW THINGS YOU SHOULD KNOW ABOUT MADDIE

**She thinks she's always right.** And she isn't. I know, because I'm never wrong. She thinks she knows best and I should just do what she says and not question her. But if I did, I'd have a bead stuck up my nose. When I was three and Maddie was four, we were playing under a table and she had one of those little plastic beads you put on your bracelet. "Watch this," she told me. She stuck it right up her nose. It was funny at first, but then it wouldn't come out. I mean, it was really up there and we got kind of scared—not that Maddie would have to go to the hospital to get it out, but that my mom would be mad at us. Just then, she sneezed, and out it popped. That was a close one, and I'm so glad I didn't follow her example.

**She pushes me in a good way.** Not many fourteen-year-olds could say they've accomplished so much at a young age. Maddie is a really hard worker. I don't know if I would ever want to work as hard as she does (it makes me tired just thinking about it), but it's shown me that you have to apply yourself. The only way to reach your goals is to put in the time and effort. My mom always tells me that, but Maddie is living proof. She's an inspiration to me.

**As far as sisters go, she's pretty cool.** Even though we're opposites. We have different styles; she usually wears jeans with Adidas, but I like to dress more sporty. She loves to dance and I like to sing (FYI, she can't carry a tune, so that's totally my thing and she can't have it). I like to have fun, and Maddie gets mad when I'm joking around and she's trying to concentrate. I think she's really good at doing hair and makeup, so I ask her to do mine. She doesn't appreciate being bothered, but eventually I'll get better at it than she is and I won't need to ask her for help anymore. Then she'll be asking me!

**We always make up.** When we are together 24/7, it's a little too much to handle and we fight. We can't help it; we get on each other's nerves. We've had some really bad fights, especially when we were younger: wrestling, hair pulling, pinching, you name it. But as we've gotten older, it's more yelling in each other's faces. We realize how silly the fights are after we've had them. A lot of our arguments are over me wanting to do stuff, and Maddie telling me no because I'm younger and she doesn't want me tagging along with her friends. Well, guess what? Everyone likes me because I'm funny and I'm fun. I think that makes her mad, because she doesn't want to think her little sister is so popular, but I can't help it—I'm very likable.

**The meanest thing she's ever done to me . . .** was kick me in the knee at a recital. I mean, seriously? The meanest thing I've ever done to her was probably just tell you that!

**She has some bad habits.** She always bites her nails and twirls her hair. I don't really have any bad habits, at least not as bad as hers.

**The one thing we have in common** is we're both obsessed with watching YouTube videos. I think I'm a little more obsessed: Last night I was up till 4 a.m. Oh, and we're both always on our phones. It drives my mom up the wall!

**The best part of being Maddie's sister** is I always have her. It's like, I'm never alone, because she's there and we have each other to hang with. A sister is like a friend you can't get rid of!

## Dear Maddie

**So my parents just told me I'm going to be a big sister. Seriously? I'm thirteen! Why would I want a baby around the house *now*? What if they ignore me when he/she comes along?**

This exact same thing happened to Kalani. It was really hard for her at first to adjust to the idea. But now her little baby brother Jett is seven months old and she is absolutely 100 percent in love with him. It's so much fun seeing them together; she FaceTimes me with him and never wants to put him down. It will take some time for you to get used to the situation as well. Your parents won't *mean* to ignore you, but a baby needs a lot of attention and it's a lot of work. So just be prepared that they may have their hands full. Make sure you tell them how you feel. They love you and they will understand and do their very best to make you okay with it. Try and think of this as a great thing that's happening in your life! I know Kalani says she can't imagine her life without baby Jett in it. He is the cutest!

**My little brother is the most annoying person on the planet. He steals my stuff and hides it, and when my friends come over he acts disgusting just to embarrass me. What should I do?**

Boys are gross in general. Your friends know that, and they're not gonna hold your brother's bad behavior against you. I, too, have a super-annoying younger sibling, and I will tell you this: The more you protest, the more obnoxious they will try to act. They want to get a reaction out of you. So my advice to you is to ignore him. He wants attention, so don't give it to him. My other suggestion is to make sure he is busy when your friends come by. Have him go on a playdate with his friends at the same time. If all else fails, bribe him to be good. Works on Kenzie every time . . .

**My parents are so unfair. They expect me to do everything because I'm the oldest, while my two younger sisters get away with murder. I can't take it anymore!**

Hmmm, this sounds familiar. My sister gets away with everything all the time. Why? Because she's younger, period. Your parents won't tell you this, but by the time your siblings came along, they were kind of over the whole "strict parent" thing. They got it out of their system with you, and they will just let your siblings slide. Personally, I just deal. I know I'm not going to win against Mackenzie, so why try? But I also know that being the oldest has its advantages: I'll get to drive a car first. I'll get to vote first. I'll get to move out on my own first. Same goes for you—your siblings will simply have to wait while you become an adult *first*. So consider yourself lucky and remind them who came first—and who always will.

## Today Is a Beautiful Day to . . .

❋ **Go tech-free.** My mom is always getting on my case: "Maddie, get off your phone!" So one day, I literally put it down all day just to see if I could survive. You know what? I actually enjoyed it. I didn't check my Instagram, I didn't read or send any texts. It felt really peaceful and freeing. I suggest picking a Saturday or a Sunday and just shutting down and tuning out. It was amazing to me how much free time I had to do other things—like organize my makeup brushes and read a pile of fashion magazines I was dying to flip through.

❋ **Dance like no one's watching.** I love to just crank up the music and let loose, not worrying about if my feet look perfect or my shoulders are straight. Dance it out!

❋ **Volunteer.** My mom has always taught me that the best gift you can give someone is your time. Pick a project, any project: an animal shelter, a home for the elderly, an after-school program at a local school. It should be something close to your heart that you feel strongly about. I'm involved with the Dancers Care

Foundation (dancerscare.org). It raises awareness and funds to help prevent cancer and ultimately find a cure, and it was created and organized by dancers and dance-related companies who recognized their power to make an impact. Once you have a group you're involved with, you can organize an event in your school to fund-raise (personally, I love a good bake sale!) and spread the word.

· *Chapter Three* ·

# LIVIN' ON THE DANCE FLOOR

$\mathcal{I}$was two when I started taking ballet. I was teeny-tiny, and I couldn't really reach the barre. All I remember doing is jumping and twirling around pretending to be a fairy princess or a butterfly—and occasionally stepping on my teacher's toes. My very first recital was this little *Nutcracker* number, and I came offstage crying. There were tears streaming down my cheeks and my mom came over to ask me what was wrong. "I want to go back onstage!" I said. I didn't want to get off the stage—I wanted to do it all over again. I guess that's when I realized that performing was "my thing," and what truly made me happy. I can't explain how or why, but I do know this: When I'm up there, looking out at an audience, it makes me feel alive.

When I was four, I started taking dance at the Abby Lee Dance Company. I knew what I wanted to sign up for: hip-hop, jazz, and tap. I told them the moment we walked in. I remember there was a big desk out front, and large studios with stars painted on the walls and tons of trophies on display. Eventually, those studios felt like they shrank in size, because I got bigger, but that first week they seemed ginormous. The ALDC teachers were probably thinking, *Who is this pip-squeak who wants to come in here and tell us what classes to put her in?* But I was always ambitious and never satisfied with dance classes that were my age level. I needed a challenge, something that I could work toward. Being in an older, more advanced group never scared me. People ask me all the time if my mom pushed me into becoming a dancer. Actually, it was me who pushed her. My mom never held me back, but she's also never been one to say, "You *have* to do this." She's supported my dreams 100 percent, but if I had changed my mind and decided I wanted to be a doctor or a lawyer or a makeup artist, she would be fine with that, too. I danced because I wanted to. I look back now and think we should have kept a tally of how much time we spent in the studio— probably hundreds and hundreds of hours. My mom never complained (well, almost never), even when she had to sit around all day and wait for me or Mackenzie to finish class or rehearsal. I wasn't aware of how many days and hours ticked by because I was working and having fun, but I bet my mom was. Dance moms are very, very patient.

In the beginning, they put me in the recreational classes instead of the company ones because of my size and age. It took a year, but I got moved up to the company when I was five. To be totally honest, I was not a good dancer. I was always the youngest, and they put me in the back of all the numbers, which made me really sad and frustrated. I didn't want to be in the background. I complained to my mom, but she told me I had to work hard and practice a lot—that was the only way to get recognized. When I first started the company tap class, the tap teacher told my mom, "She's too young but she can sit and watch in the back." I did what he asked, but as I stared from the sidelines, I moved my feet along to the choreography he was teaching—and nailed it. So he changed his mind pretty quickly and let me join in. That was always what happened. I didn't have the best dance technique, but I was really good at picking up the choreography. If you showed me a step once, I could do it. Maybe I couldn't do it perfectly, but I could do it.

Slowly, I got moved to the middle and then the front of all the group dances. It didn't happen overnight; I had to work my butt off. My teachers used to always say, "Sometimes it's not the best dancer who succeeds in showbiz but the one who works the hardest." Well, that's me—the one who worked super hard. If it had all come easily to me, if I'd been born with natural talent, maybe I wouldn't have felt the way I did. Maybe I would have gotten bored and moved on to something more challenging. But the fact that I wasn't very good to begin with made me want it even more.

I started doing tap solos and taking classes regularly. I took tap for a very long time—it was one of the first styles I fell in love with. I liked creating "music" and rhythm with my feet. It's like you're an instrument playing along with the song. A tap dance can look fast and frenzied to the audience, but it requires such control and precision to keep the taps clean. My teacher built me up and gave me so much confidence. He didn't seem to notice how small or young I was; he just saw that I wanted so badly to dance and I had a passion for it.

I started competing when I was five. I did a ballet solo, then a tap solo, and I lost both. I remember at the time thinking I did pretty well—I earned high gold, and that sounded like a gold medal in the Olympics to me. But the goal was to get platinum. The next year, when I was six, I started going to different competitions and conventions. I won and I kept winning. I remember this really cute tap dance I did to "Sunshine and Lollipops" from the movie *Cloudy with a Chance of Meatballs*. It was at a Jump competition in Pittsburgh and I was seven. I had this big pink bow on my head and I made all these kissy-faces! Soon I was piling up trophies (one that was six feet tall!), ribbons, plaques, and medals—eventually too many for the display case and shelves in my bedroom to hold.

When I was eight, I had my first lyrical solo in a competition: "Cry." It was actually supposed to be called "Somewhere over the Rainbow," but at the last minute we had to change it for some copyright reason. People ask me a lot what the craziest part of competing is. I'd have to say it's the element of surprise. Something always changes, goes wrong, tears, or breaks down. I've had my music skip, my props drop, and I've literally had to be sewn into costumes several times when the zipper or clasp broke just minutes before going onstage. Things happen—that's the only given. And the more you compete, the more you learn to roll with it. I've always thought that in some way that's a great life lesson: Don't count on things going the way you think they will. The key is to be prepared for whatever curve ball comes at you. In the beginning, my teammates and I would freak out, but by the end of my time with ALDC, it took a lot to throw me. I've learned that great dancers exhibit grace under pressure. When your headpiece flies off, when the music stops playing, that's when you really prove what you're made of.

When I joined the junior elite team, I thought it was going to be awesome. I loved being on a stage; I loved being a member of a group and feeling part of something bigger than myself. I really had no idea what to expect; I thought it would all be fun—the hair, the makeup, the sparkly costumes, traveling around to lots of different cities. I saw the older girls who competed, and they looked so grown-up and glamorous—I wanted to be like them. But as I got older, the competitions got much more intense. The fierce competitive side of all this was something I never saw coming. Through it all, our team stayed tight and tried to focus on us, not on what other teams were doing or saying, but it was hard. People ask me a lot if what they see on *Dance Moms* is real, i.e., the fighting with other teams and between moms and coaches. Well, I can't really answer that—I don't watch the show. I've probably only seen one entire episode from start to finish. I don't love watching myself—it's kind of weird and I feel like, "Well, that's behind me now." I lived through it, so why do I need to watch it happen all over again? But I can tell you that competitions are stressful, and things can and do get ugly sometimes because people don't behave like good sports. So yeah, sometimes people go a little crazy. But through it all, my teammates and I had each other's backs, and if there was disappointment—if someone forgot a step or we lost first place to a rival team—

there was no one person to blame. We were all responsible; one for all, all for one. Losing isn't fun; no one *wants* to lose. But it happens a lot, and to everyone. Even if I was on a winning streak, I might have an off day and come in second or third or not even place. Because you won the weekend before doesn't mean you'll win this time—it's never a given. And if you lose, it doesn't mean you're a bad dancer or a bad person. It just means it was a bad day.

I'm a perfectionist, so especially in the beginning of my competition days, I would go over and over every dance in my head and pick out the parts that weren't right—sometimes tiny details no one else would notice, but I just *knew* weren't as good as they could be. I would dwell on the mistakes instead of focusing on what I had done right; I would pick apart every dance, even though my teammates and coaches were telling me I did a great job.

I think it was just because I was young and inexperienced; I didn't know better. I didn't see the value in not winning, how it drives you and makes you work harder. So that was a really tough thing for me to learn—to let go and forgive myself for being human and messing up. I think what finally made the difference was expanding my horizons. The more things I did—like acting in movies and TV and making videos—the less competitive dancing defined me. I didn't feel like it was the end of the world anymore if I didn't take home a first-place trophy. I had other things going on in my life, and I was able to keep it in perspective. But I did a lot of crying in those early competitions. My nerves were really bad, because I felt so much was riding on every single number we performed. If you watch me in the wings, you'll always see me biting my nails—Kenzie's right about that habit of mine!

I put a lot of that pressure on myself; I didn't want to disappoint anyone—my teachers, my teammates, my mom, our audience—and I was so insecure in my talent and abilities back then. When I think back on it now, I was a different person. This Maddie has much more confidence and doesn't need a title to feel good about herself. I actually like to lose sometimes—it's like someone is lighting a match under me, firing me up for next time.

There were many, many times I had to push through and compete, even if I was feeling sick. I remember I once had bronchitis and I could barely breathe without coughing, but I had a solo and a group number to get through. I literally had to hold my breath through the numbers so I wouldn't start a coughing fit. I haven't loved every dance we've done—some I thought were a little weird or silly, or even inappropriate for kids our age. My favorites are always the emotionally charged ones that really speak to the audience. If I had to pick my least favorite dance, I would say "This Girl's Gotta Be Kissed," a musical theater duet I did with Gino Cosculluela. I was eleven at the time, and to this day, it remains the most embarrassing, humiliating moment of my life! I had to kiss a boy in front of millions on national TV. There was no marking it; every time we rehearsed, we had to actually lock lips. Gino and I were friends who kind of crushed on each other—but then this dance totally cured me of that. I didn't even want to think about the dance, because I was mortified. My mom says you always should learn something from a new experience, so here's what I learned: If I can survive this, I can survive anything. It was the most miserable week for me, and I couldn't wait for it to be over. Maybe I am being a little overly dramatic, but I'd rather have a root canal than relive it.

Drama seems to go hand in hand with being on a reality TV show. Not a lot of competitive dancers have to deal with cameras on them 24/7. At first it was weird, but it didn't bother me—I was eight years old at the time, and there were cameramen following me around everywhere I went. I would just ignore them and go about my business. Eventually, you feel a little exposed because you're "on" all the time. Your life is what the show is about, but you're also trying to live it. I just wanted to dance; I didn't want all the drama. As soon as

*Dance Moms* aired in July of 2011, we became reality TV personalities, and everywhere we went, especially in the dance competition world, people recognized us. Two million people tuned in every week; that's a lot of people watching. We started to get a big fan following. I remember one of our first appearances in a mall in Westchester, New York. It was me, Mackenzie, Chloe Lukasiak, and our moms, and we expected maybe a few dozen fans to show up. We were dancing and also modeling in a kids' fashion runway show. Well, we got to the mall and it was crazy: a thousand screaming fans, pushing and shoving and trying to get close to us. Where did all these people come from? It was pretty scary, and they had to call extra security. We actually had to hide locked in a store for a while till the crowds thinned out and the screaming stopped. Afterward, we still sat there for hours, signing photos and posing for selfies. I was only about nine, so I didn't really know what to make of all the attention; I thought it was a little weird. I mean, why were these people so excited to see us? It's not like we were the cast of *iCarly* or something. *That* I would understand. I remember asking my mom, "Is this all for us?" and she nodded yes. Her eyes were wide and she looked shocked, too.

When it came to competing, being recognized was a good thing but also had its downside; people expected us to be the best because we were the ones with the TV show. That was a lot of pressure—we had a reputation to live up to. Sometimes it felt like we had to prove ourselves over and over again. But we had our moms there to remind us that winning wasn't everything; what was more important was the fact that we were learning and growing as dancers, and that we gave it our all. My mom cried whenever I cried, but she helped me shake it off and move on—I'm stronger because of her pep talks. I honestly don't know how I would have handled it all without her being there—not to mention my teammates, who became my best friends. I love them all and we have a special bond that comes around once in a lifetime. We cheer each other on; we support each other's dreams—it goes way beyond our team. They're really my family and I know we'll be in each other's lives forever. There isn't a day that goes by that I don't text several if not all of them (JoJo is Snapchatting me right now). I had my last competition in Vegas this past summer, and it felt sad, like a chapter in my life was ending. I'm excited to be moving on, to be doing other things beyond competing, but there is part of me that will miss it. It was my childhood. It was all I knew for so many years. I was in the studio more than I was in my own home.

A lot of crazy stuff happened over the course of those years competing—stuff you don't get to see on TV but that we all lived through and experienced. Like the time our team bus broke down on the side of the road in California en route to a competition the next day. It was blazing hot, and we had to walk on the highway to find a place to get something to eat. We cheered when we found a Panda Express Chinese restaurant, and ordered practically everything on the menu. It took nearly three hours for them to send a new bus to rescue us. My mom was convinced we would be sleeping in Panda Express—or on the side of the road—that night!

There was also a lot of last-minute costume creating that went on. All the dance moms would gather in my mom's hotel room on the Friday before competition weekend and start gluing and sewing our outfits. Sometimes I wouldn't even get mine till fifteen minutes before I had to go on and perform—and I was praying it would fit. I remember one time the moms were handed a sports bra and booty shorts and told, "Make a cowboy outfit." My mom scratched her head: "Out of this?" They always had to be really creative and have a hot glue gun ready to go. Sometimes, things come apart at the seams: I had this cute tap number, "You and Me Against the World," where I was wearing a pink apron. The ribbon around my neck came undone and the apron started to fall down in the middle of the number. I just kept going. I figured if I stopped, I'd miss a step, so I kept tapping with only half a costume.

The nights before competition we stayed in the hotel—which was like having a giant slumber party. We would all get together in one room, get into our PJs, and order room service while our moms would go downstairs to the restaurant and hang out together. Girl bonding on both sides! I remember one time our moms came up after dinner, and we were all dancing around with travel pillows on our heads in the shower making videos. We have a lot of fun ways of blowing off steam. Kendall and I like to choreograph dances with our hands! Seriously, we would be sitting on a plane on a long flight somewhere, and we would use our fingers to dance across the folding food tray. And sometimes backstage waiting to go on and compete, we will do runway walks in the dressing room—but walking on our hands! When we were waiting for the grand opening ceremony at L.A. ALDC, we jumped out our pent-up energy on the trampoline in one of the studios. A lot goes on in that studio! Kenzie learned to ride her hoverboard there, and I took my first spin as well—Kendall had to hold my hands while I screamed, "I'm scared! I'm gonna fall!" But eventually we got it. We've also been known to break out into some spontaneous silly dances when rehearsals get a bit too intense—like the Whip/Nae Nae and the Macarena or some crazy improv moves (we just make sure none of our teachers are watching!). I also recall a competition in Vegas where we got our hands on some silly string—and decided to let it fly to celebrate our group dance win. The only way to balance out the stress of competing is to get wild and wacky. Looking back on those times, they're some of my favorite memories with my team—which our moms usually manage to capture on video to remind us how crazy we are!

## Memories of Maddie

"One of my favorite memories is [of] the day Maddie and I randomly made up a song called 'Monarch.' I don't know why we find that song so funny, but every time we sing the song we start cracking up with laughter. When we're not dancing, we love to bake together. She usually comes to my house around Christmas and we bake, watch movies, and love pulling pranks on my brothers. She is the same Maddie that I have always known. She is dedicated and consistent. We know and understand each other. I miss her a lot and so does the team, but we understand her need to branch out. It is different not having Maddie there to tell her funny jokes." —Nia Sioux

"Nia and Maddie were friends before kindergarten, before the television show. They are two Pittsburgh girls who shared a passion for dance. After a decade of being together for hours almost every day, it was a significant change not having them around. We remain connected. They may not talk every day, but when they see each other they can pick up where they left off. Sometimes they share a moment without words—a smile or a giggle conveys a lot. They understand each other. They each want the best for each other, and they are very supportive of each other. Scheduling can be difficult but each of the girls makes it a point to congratulate the other when she achieves a milestone.

"I do not think they can remember a time when they were not friends. We toured Europe, Australia, and America together. We met incredible people on our adventures and experienced new cultures, foods, and sights. Going to the Eiffel Tower, holding a koala, and taking countless bus rides were part of our journey. It was so special sharing these moments with our daughters. [Maddie's mom] Melissa and I love reading, so we had our own little book club! I have fond memories of our discussions. Maddie has a positive energy that is contagious. Her confidence, hard work, and diligence are a great example to young girls. Maddie's journey was unique and illustrates that you have to put in the hard work to achieve a dream."

—Holly Frazier (Nia's mom)

\* \* \*

I remember almost every dance I did—what I wore, what the music was, where and when we danced it. I could even probably still do the choreography: It's etched on my brain! In all, there were probably over two hundred dance competitions I competed in. Honestly, I've lost track—I'd have to probably check the *Dance Moms* fan pages for a complete list. My mom is pretty funny—she blocks this stuff out. I do a dance and she forgets it immediately—like on the bus on the way home. She has to literally go through racks of costumes in our "costume room" at home or watch the episodes on YouTube to jog her memory. There have just been so, so many, but when I connect with a dance, I feel like it becomes a part of me. And then I can never forget.

# *My Most Memorable Dances*

**"Cry."** The song was by Alexx Calise, who is one of my favorite singer/songwriters. My first lyrical solo ever at a StarQuest competition. It's kind of a sad song: "I don't wanna do anything but cry . . ." Very sad lyrics, and my mom cried her eyes out watching me do it—I could actually see her sobbing in the front row! But I was trying to be very free and happy in my dancing—like I had to rise above all the storms and darkness. My costume was supposed to look like Dorothy from *The Wizard of Oz*. Kenzie did the solo years later and wore the same costume for it, and I have to say she was amazing.

**"Vertigo."** I performed this at Sheer Talent. Rachael Sage wrote the music; she does almost all of my solo songs, and I love her voice and the way she captures emotion in song. This was an intense one: "Every time I hold your hand it feels like I'm drowning." The character had to be someone in pain, trying to escape, but she keeps being pulled back. I remember the choreography had a lot of spinning, because when you have vertigo, you're dizzy.

**"Timeless."** I performed this solo at Masters of Dance Arts. The artist is Cassandra Kubinski. It's about love that never ends, and I like how simple my costume was—just this pale blue halter top with a little skirt. Sometimes less is more. A really overdone costume with lots of trim and glitter can sometimes distract from the dancing (in my humble opinion!). Love is a really popular theme for competition music, which is kind of funny when you think about it. How many tweens and teens have experienced a broken heart or "love that explodes then burns out?" You have to really use your imagination and get into the character; you have to feel the loss in a very mature way. Sometimes these lyrics scare me—is that what being in a relationship will be like? Getting your heart broken in a million pieces then being swallowed up in pain and regret? Doesn't sound too appealing!

**"Birthday."** Rachael Sage again at Sheer Talent again! It starts off with me blowing out the candles on an imaginary cake. It's mostly happy, but there are moments of frustration and sadness—especially at the end. I love how it switches back and forth emotionally like that; like someone is flipping a switch. It's really an acting challenge. And the purple costume with all the floaty layers is really beautiful when I do my turns.

**"Happiness."** I did this at Energy last minute and also

at Believe nationals. It's a Rachael Sage song again about things getting better; happiness where there was once sadness, love lifting you up. Really pretty pink costume and I just felt good doing it—happy!

**"Come to the Cabaret."** I love the glittery theatrical costume and how sassy this dance was. Really fun, but a little nerve-racking: I learned this jazz solo a day before the Masters of Dance Arts competition! The song was by We3Kings and it had this Broadway feel to it. I loved getting into this character—she's having fun because "life is a cabaret dance."

**"All God's Creatures."** If I had to pick one favorite solo, this is probably it for a lot of reasons. First of all, Rachael Sage wrote the music and it's really powerful. I won first place with it at Energy nationals. I play a homeless girl, and the costume was some Kmart clothes we shredded up into rags and a shawl pinned over my head. It was shabby, not chic. I love the makeup, too: my eyes look all sunken in, like I haven't slept in weeks. I'm kind of tortured throughout this contemporary dance, struggling to survive. I think it really touches the audience and allows them to feel what it must be like to be homeless and helpless on the street.

**"Lizzie Borden."** Wacky. Really weird. This was before I loved horror movies, at the New York Dance Experience competition. My character is a crazy, bloody killer running around with a hatchet. My costume was a white blood-stained apron, and my makeup was demonic. I scared myself looking in the mirror. Whenever I go to bed before the day of a competition, I run my solo like nine hundred times. I kept playing the music by Louise Heaney over and over. This eerie voice repeats over and over again, "He's behind you!" Can you imagine the nightmares I had?

**"The Game of Love."** Loved it. Loved the costume, especially the tie with the heart on it. Loved the music. My mom says it sounded like an old Frank Sinatra song (but it was really by L. J. Nachsin). Love tapping! It's just so much fun for me, and I don't have to be in my head as much—it comes naturally. I just move through the dance, having the best time. I feel like the smiles are real. That was World-Class Talent and also the same competition where Mackenzie was doing "Cry." She went on right after me, and when I saw her in the wings I gave her advice: "Point your toes, straighten your legs." Then I hugged her and said, "I love you." She nailed it, as I knew she would.

**"Two Sapphires."** My first duet with Kalani at Sheer Talent in New York. It was so us: "two shooting stars, two lightning storms . . ." Our birthdays are in September, a week apart, and our birthstone is sapphire, so it had a lot of meaning for us. Kalani is such a gorgeous technical dancer, and she pushed me to meet her there. One of my favorite duets ever, because I felt like we were so in sync, both in the dance and emotionally, too.

**"Sugar and Spice."** Upbeat and cute—it was the first time Kendall and I danced a duet together. I had a solo the week before, and I know I was supposed to feel bad that I didn't have a solo this week, but we just couldn't stop laughing together. We wore these brown sparkly costumes that looked like brown sugar, but hers was jazz and mine was a ballerina tutu. I love our energy when we dance together. I feel like we play off each other so well and bring out the best in each other. We have this incredible chemistry that's hard to explain; we just "get" each other.

**"The Last Text."** This is the one that *Dance Moms* fans seem to always talk about. It was incredibly powerful, a warning about texting and driving. We performed it at Energy nationals. We were all in party dresses, and Paige Hyland was supposed to be driving us. We had to act like we were all busy texting and gabbing and then there's this huge CRASH and we all kind of roll out of the car and wind up dead on the ground. I'm the only one who survives as Paige slumps over the wheel. It was silent when we finished; no one knew whether to clap or cry or scream. It was that shocking; you felt like you had just witnessed a tragic car accident. I'm really proud of this dance because it had such an important message and an incredible impact on anyone who watched it. I hope it saves lives.

**"Amber Alert."** Another really dramatic group dance we did, this time at In10sity Dance. Kenzie plays a little girl who is kidnapped (by Nia!). The music is really haunting: "No one will take you, I'll keep you whole until I die . . ." At the end, I find Kenzie dead in a chair and I run offstage crying. I had to really go to a place where I could imagine my little sister in danger. I think of it today and I get chills. It was so dark and eerie because it's real; kids are taken every day. Sometimes the scariest dances are the ones about real situations, not fantasies. Not a lot of dance competition teams do these kinds of dances—they're sort of a *Dance Moms* thing. But even if they're scary or bloody, I like a dance that tells a story or leaves the audience thinking.

**"The Waiting Room."** We did this at Center Stage nationals and it's my favorite group dance ever, although I think I'm still traumatized from it. We're supposed to be sitting in a hospital waiting room, worrying, watching the clock tick away on the wall as the hours go by. Nia is in surgical scrubs covered in blood; each of us waits for the word: Who lives and who dies? I have to walk to the corner of the stage, shaking my head in disbelief. I finally get the horrible news that someone I love is gone, and I crumble. I was physically shaken in that moment. If I watch it over again, I actually feel that horrible hole in my heart; that pit in my stomach, as if it's real and it's happening and I'm helpless to stop it. The tears were real; the pain was real. I was in that moment.

# ⚮ MY TEAMMATES ⚮

I remember the very first moments I met each of my ALDC friends like it was yesterday . . .

*Nia:* I was about four years old the first time I saw her in the studio at ALDC. She used to wear these curly pigtails and they were so cute. She's a year older than me, and I was very impressed because whenever we would go to dance conventions, she would win all these scholarships because she was so sassy and such a great performer. Our favorite thing to do together was have sleepovers at both our homes in Pittsburgh. We had our traditions. She got a baking set once for Christmas, so we would bake up a storm: cupcakes, cookie cakes, brownies, you name it. And we would make Video Stars on the app. We would dance and lip-synch to a lot of songs by Katy Perry! I knew even back then Nia was going to be a pop star—the girl can really sing. Just recently, Nia came to see me at one of the Sia concerts and I was so happy. She's one of those people who it doesn't matter how long it's been since you've seen each other, you just pick up where you left off. She's the one friend that I always trust the most. I can tell her my biggest secrets and she will always keep them.

*Kendall:* I was the first one she met when she came to our studio. She was sitting by herself, looking a little lost, and I said, "Come over and hang out with me." Over the years, we've had a lot of crazy things we invented to do together—like the soap trampoline. We would pour liquid dish soap all over the trampoline in her backyard, then hit it with a hose. You slip and slide all over it, and at some point, you can't even stand up and there are bubbles everywhere. At her house, we played a lot of GarageBand, creating these hilarious mashups and choreographing dances to them. We'd call in Kendall's sisters, parents, grandparents, and there'd be twelve people watching us put on a show. I think my favorite mashup of all time was the "PB and J Time" song (don't ask!). If Kendall is reading this, she's rolling on the floor laughing . . .

She also had a golf cart that was at her nan's house. The backyard had three acres (it used to be a farm), and her grandma used it to get around. We would drive it around, and Kendall was really good at it. One day, we were going to a grad party in the neighborhood with Nia and decided to take the cart to get there.

"You wanna drive?" Kendall asked Nia. "It's really fun and easy."

Nia hesitated for a second—she'd never driven a golf cart before. "Um, sure."

She got behind the wheel and was literally inching down the street, barely moving at all. At this rate, we were never going to get to the party.

"Come on, you can go a little faster!" we teased her. "You're driving like a granny." Famous last words! She hit the gas and didn't know how to turn or stop. Kendall and I were praying for our lives! Finally, she went flying into someone's driveway, almost hitting a brick wall, and slammed on the brakes. Lesson learned: Do not let Nia behind a wheel without a lot more practice!

*Kalani:* We met when she was doing Abby's Ultimate and clicked. She's super fun, and always honest with me—which I love. I can ask her, "Is this outfit cute?" and she'll say, "Um, not your best look," and we'll crack up. She has a brand-new car, a white Range Rover, which she got for her birthday before she even had her license! I went with her and her mom, Kira, to the DMV when she took her road test. I was filming all of Kalani's three-point turns on my phone, cheering her on. Then she got out of the car with this sad look on her face.

"Oh no! Did you fail?" My heart was pounding, because I knew how much this meant to her.

Suddenly, her face lit up and she grinned from ear to ear. "Nope! I passed! Gotcha!" She's such an amazing friend, and I can always count on her for everything.

*JoJo:* The girl is literally a ball of energy—completely crazy, but in a great way that lights up a room. She joined ALDC after doing Abby's Ultimate and truly ended up one of my best friends. We share an obsession for *Grey's Anatomy*, but she has taken hers to a whole other level, and I don't just mean binge-watching thirteen seasons over the past three months. She actually went on eBay and bought scrubs and a name tag that reads DR. SIWA. I'm not kidding; I'm actually a little scared she's going to wear it out in public. My mom and I love her and her mom, Jessalyn; they are the sweetest, kindest people, and so supportive. I FaceTime JoJo constantly— I just need my daily dose of her to make me laugh. I keep asking her when she's gonna retire the giant bows and she tells me, "Yeah, soon." But I've seen her hair accessory collection and it's not going to be easy. We might have to surgically remove them . . .

## *Memories of Maddie*

"I first had Maddie in a ballet class when she was five years old. She would stand in the back corner and not say a word. Sometimes her belly would hurt and she would come whisper that to me. I always told her she could sit down and take a break, but she never wanted to. She wasn't the best in the class, but I could always tell she was listening and taking everyone else's corrections. One day, we were doing a *petit allegro* and she asked if we landed one of the jumps on the eight or the one. At that point, I knew this five-year-old was something special. I didn't even know the exact counts myself!

"The first dance I worked on with Maddie was her very first solo, 'I Want to Be a Star.' We cleaned it every Tuesday for a half hour. She knew the routine like the back of her hand. Every correction I'd give her she would over-exaggerate, fixing it so I would notice. More vividly, I can remember transforming 'Over the Rainbow' into 'Cry' for the TV show. She had *à la seconde* turns to a double pir-ouette at the end of the routine that were a little rough that we worked on forever! Her timing and stage presence were impeccable from the beginning.

"Every Tuesday, come rain or shine, 4 p.m. to 4:30 p.m. was our time slot. That time slot went to learning how to come up from a backbend to creating routines like 'She's History,' which is one of my favorites. We would work on cleaning her dances, making up combos, and later on creating routines once *Dance Moms* hit. I can remember seeing Maddie pacing back and forth in the doorway until 4 p.m. As soon as I let my prior student out, she would bust through the door—couldn't wait another minute. We would be dripping sweat, both of us, by the end of the lesson. No matter what we did, she was dancing 150 percent every time and giving every ounce of energy she had. She was always so polite. She would thank me a million times for the smallest things. She would open up to me in our private rehearsals, but kept more to herself when it came time for other classes. She has definitely grown up, but I still see the same little Maddie.

"I have so many fun memories with her! During the summer of Season 1 we were attending several nationals that came through the city. We were filming at one of them, and then our other company kids were competing at two additional ones. Of course, Maddie was involved in all three. As soon as she competed her solo at the first, she and I got in a taxi. I completely changed her costume head to toe and her hairstyle by the time we got down the Vegas strip to the next competition. The driver had no idea. We jumped out, we ran through the casino, and she was next onstage!

"Maddie always excels in the group routines. In a lot of them she was the lead, which put a lot more pressure on her. I can remember us doing a routine called 'War Torn.' In rehearsal she said to me, 'I think this is the fastest choreography you've ever given me.' Of course she was nailing it, but in the end, I thought it was too fast and choppy and wound up slowing it down. So she was right! I think 'Vertigo' ranks up there as one of her hardest solos. I remember thinking, *Whoa, that's a lot of tricks!* Also, the number we did for a young girl who is part of the Starlight [Children's] Foundation called 'Hold On' was pretty difficult.

"The numbers I feel are Maddie's strength are the dark instrumental pieces, like 'Lizzie Borden' or 'Hostage.' She makes those pieces more than just dance steps: She pulls you into her world. Most of the themes and songs are chosen by the producers. However, I have access to the music databases that we use so I can go in and choose some myself. If I find something that really jumps out to me for a certain girl on the team, I will pitch it to the producers and then they will create a story or theme around that piece of music. I usually steer toward lyrical or contemporary because that is what I feel I am best at, but an audience that isn't as familiar with dance would think that was boring, which is why we cover all styles on the show. ALDC is known for their dark, contemporary pieces that really tell a story and leave you wanting more.

"The kids were so young in the beginning of *Dance Moms*, I don't really think they saw what was happening. As they grew up, the followers grew and now they—and the show—are HUGE. I think Maddie's social media following goes up every time I look at her pages. She's the best role model a teen can ask for—she's such a hard worker, gives 150 percent to everything she does, and always keeps a smile on her face. We are still very close! We went to lunch about a month ago, and it's always just like old times. We show each other different routines/combos and stuff we see online, gossip about anything, and of course, shop! She snuck me around backstage at the Sia tour and I got to give her a big squeeze and say, 'Be good!' as I normally would before she would go out to perform in competition.

"I think the sky is the limit for Maddie. I always knew she'd be successful, I just didn't realize it would all happen so quickly. I think she's absolutely on the right path, and if she keeps it up, she's going to be unstoppable. What am I talking about? She already is!"—Gianna Martello

## Dear Maddie

**I just found out my friend is talking about me behind my back, making fun of me to other kids in my school. I thought we were close, but I guess not! I feel totally stabbed in the back.**

I don't blame you! I've been the victim of a "frenemy" several times. I've made the mistake of thinking some girls were nice, only to find out they were dissing me to other people. Before you let people into your circle, be sure that you can trust them. Friendships—at least really good ones—take time, and you should get to know someone well before you open up to him or her. I've had to weed out a bunch of fake friends, and it's not fun. The best advice I can give you is to notice how people are around you: Do they confide in you? Offer to lend a hand when you need help or an ear when you're stressed or upset? Or do they exclude you and say insulting things, then laugh, "Just kidding?" In my book, that's a sure sign of a phony who's not worthy of your time.

**I think my friend has an eating disorder. She never eats lunch in the school cafeteria and she's lost a lot of**

**weight. What should I do? I don't want to get her in trouble!**

You don't want her to suffer either—or worse, wind up in the hospital or dead. I'm sorry if that sounds harsh, but eating disorders are serious health issues and should never be ignored. Have you asked her what's going on? Told her you're worried about her? If she denies there's a problem but you still see one, as much as it might make her mad or upset with you, you have to tell her parents or an adult at school about your concerns. If my friend was in danger, I'd let someone know *fast* before the situation got any worse. I'd say, "Listen, I love you and this is why I want you to get help." Eventually, she'll understand why you did what you did and she'll realize what a good friend you are.

**I am so stressed out! I have homework, tests, and Sunday school, on top of my dance classes five times a week. No one understands how I feel!**

I do—this sounds a lot like my life. My schedule has always been crazy, but I've learned how to manage and juggle a lot of balls without feeling too overwhelmed. Honestly, the key is to get super organized. Mark everything down on a calendar or planner; set alarms and reminders

$\mathcal{M}$adison Nicole Ziegler. Wasn't I cute?

$\mathcal{A}$n Easter surprise!

$\mathcal{M}$om, me, and Kenzie

$\mathcal{I}$ ♥ Kenzie so much.

$\mathcal{E}$aster.

Look how far we've come!

My first tap costume.

# Always leaping.

*I*'ve worn some crazy costumes over the years.

All in a day's work!

$\mathcal{I}$was
always
performing . . .

And sometimes it paid off!

 Sunshine and Lollipops.

$\mathcal{W}$e love having fun.

$\mathcal{I}$ was such a little nugget, lol.

*K*ennywood for Gia's birthday.

*K*alani always
supports me.

I've
always
loved
animals.

Cleland
Wildlife Park

𝒜mazing memories that I will never forget.

*M*y girls.

on your phone; make sure you know when things are due and what's coming up. Make to-do lists and check them off. If you still feel like you're drowning, you can always ask someone for help—your parents, your siblings, your friends, your teachers. You're not in this alone. That said, you also need to consider whether you're spreading yourself too thin. Do you love dance, and are you willing to be in a studio that many days and hours? If the answer is yes, then go for it. I'd personally rather be busy than bored at home watching TV. But if it's not truly your passion (or it was once but isn't anymore), it's okay to cut back and give yourself a breather.

*Today Is a Beautiful Day to . . .*

✻ **Mismatch something you're wearing**—your socks, your earrings, your gold and silver jewelry. Just to mix things up a little!

✻ **Sneak in some exercise.** We live on the third floor of our apartment complex in L.A., and most of the time we're lazy and take the elevator. But if I climb the stairs, I'm getting in exercise when I didn't even think I had time to work out. Yay me!

✻ **Paint a picture.** Remember when you were in kindergarten and the most fun part of every day was getting to finger paint on an easel? Get out a piece of paper and a paint set and just let your brush wander across the page. Paint whatever comes to mind—it doesn't have to be a masterpiece. For me, it just gets my creativity flowing.

· Chapter Four ·

## IT'S JUST ME

*P*eople sometimes come up to me and stare; they forget that I'm a person. When this happens, I don't really know what to do. I usually smile and say, "Hi, what's your name?" and hope they snap out of it. Seriously, I have been in airports or restaurants or strolling around L.A., face-to-face with someone who has seen me on TV, and they just stand there, speechless—or worse, they cry. They actually cry! I get what that feels like—if I bumped into Ellen Pompeo or Blake Lively or even a Kardashian/Jenner I might be tongue-tied, too. When I recently met Ashley Tisdale (aka Sharpay) backstage at *So You Think You Can Dance*, I was so happy.

It's so sweet when people recognize me, but they don't re-alize that I have a life just like them. Take today: I've literally been in my sweatpants and T-shirt all day. I think I slept in them, too. My mom had to beg me to change out of them so we could go out to dinner with friends who are visiting us from Pittsburgh. I pulled on a ripped pair of jeans and a plain black slouchy tee and put my hair up in a messy bun. Don't tell her, but I didn't even brush it. I'm not wearing any makeup, and although my mom's nails are long and mani-cured Barbie pink, mine are short and stubby and unpolished. So glam, right? Unless I am going out to an event where I'm going to be mobbed by cameras on the red carpet, this is me—a pretty normal teenager and kind of low-maintenance.

I work so much that I like my days off to be stress-free: completely chilling out, sleeping late, ordering in, and not getting dressed up or even dressed at all beyond my PJs. I might binge-watch three episodes of *Grey's* on Netflix to catch up so JoJo won't spoil it for me—this is what happens when your friends are a season ahead. We are so addicted. We went online and ordered matching sweatshirts that say all the interns' names and another one that says IT'S A BEAUTIFUL DAY TO SAVE LIVES. But sometimes JoJo gets a little carried away. The other day she FaceTimed me and showed me her iPad screen.

"Look at what's happening! I'm so devastated!" She zoomed in on one of the characters getting shot. "I can't! I just can't!" she cried.

Click! Just like that, she hung up, leaving me to deal with the horror of that image she'd just shared—of McDreamy, one of my fave doctors on the show, fighting for his life. I had no idea how many seasons it would take me to find out if he survived. Are you kidding me? I was so mad, I made her promise to let me catch up before she blurted anything else out. So I'm still somewhere in the middle of Season 3, dreading the Mc-Dreamy shooting coming up in Season 6. Thanks, JoJo. It's like skipping to the last page of a novel and finding out it's going to end really, really badly.

No day in L.A. is really "typical" for me, because stuff seems to always come up—there might be a meeting or audition that just appears out of thin air. We try to keep to a schedule, but things are always changing. That's L.A. Traffic is slow, but everything else here moves really fast. When I'm back home in Pittsburgh, it feels much calmer and life is more of a routine. I'll usually sleep till nine or ten. I am *not* a morning person, and my friends know not to text me till noon. I'm grumpy if you wake me. I'll go downstairs and make myself breakfast—usually a smoothie or a bowl of Cap'n Crunch with berries. If I had my way, I'd have ice cream for breakfast, but my mom doesn't appreciate that. She can't seem to understand that Ben & Jerry's is a basic food group.

I usually hang with my neighbors at our pool or on their trampoline, though we might go shopping. My friend Sydney is seventeen and has her license, so she can drive us to the mall or to the Shop 'n Save. The other day, we went shopping for recipe ingredients. We found a Buffalo chicken dip recipe somewhere online and decided to improvise our own version. It was amazing. I ate so many tortilla chips and veggies smothered in our dip (actually, I might have scraped some right out of the bowl with a spoon, too), I felt like I was going to explode. There are always scented candles burning in my home. I always have to feel like my house smells nice, the opposite of the stinky, smelly dance studios. I feel like the odor of sweat, armpits, and dirty feet clings to everything, so candles are the only way to get rid of it.

# ⚹ BEST BUFFALO CHICKEN DIP EVER ⚹

A yummy appetizer for a girlfriend get-together—and so easy to make

Ingredients

- *1 package (8 oz.) cream cheese, softened*
- *1 can (12 oz.) chunk white chicken, drained (you can also use chopped-up leftover roast chicken—about 1–2 cups)*
- *½ cup Buffalo wing sauce (my friends prefer it spicy!)*
- *½ cup ranch dressing*
- *2 cups shredded cheese (you can go for something like a spicy Havarti, Colby, even cheddar—whatever you like most)*

Preheat oven to 350 degrees. Spread cream cheese on the bottom of an ungreased baking dish. We used one of my mom's that's rectangular and shallow and holds about a quart. On top of the cream cheese, layer your chicken. Then place wing sauce on top, and salad dressing on top of that. Finally, sprinkle cheese on top and bake until you see all the cheese melted and bubbly. It should take about 20 minutes; any longer and it might burn, so keep an eye on it. Go ahead and dip your chips in it; it's pretty delicious on anything—even bread or a pretzel.

# ⚹ MADDIE'S MORNING SMOOTHIE ⚹

So I don't have an official ingredient list for this. I just throw in whatever fruit we have in our L.A. apartment, whatever my mom might have picked up at the farmers' market. Usually, it's strawberries, bananas, blueberries, and raspberries—all kinds of berries in general. You can always do frozen if you don't have fresh. I'll toss a handful or two into my Magic Bullet blender along with ⅓ cup cranberry or apple juice. If you like your smoothie thick, you can add ¼ cup yogurt, but I'm really not a Greek-yogurt girl (although I know it's good for you). Blend until smooth.

For the record, there are no decent clothing stores in Pittsburgh. Even the mall is underwhelming. L.A. has spoiled me. The Grove is the best thing in the entire world, in case you're wondering. It has every single store I love, from Brandy Melville, Nordstrom, Topshop and Sephora, to Dylan's Candy Bar and Sprinkles Cupcakes. Pittsburgh just pales in comparison. It's not its fault: Hollywood is a hard act to follow.

When we're back in Pittsburgh, we eat at home a lot, because we're basically never home—this is our chance. My stepdad Greg will grill up a steak or chicken, or we'll order in from Azan Wok—the best Chinese food that's five minutes from our house, so it takes no time at all to deliver. My mom orders from them so much that they recognize her voice on the phone: "You want the usual? Chicken on a stick?" That's not what it's even called (it says "chicken skewers" on the menu), but that's what my mom has named it. We'll get some edamame on the side; I'll get white rice and Kenzie will get fried rice, whatever we're in the mood for. If we're starved, we'll eat right out of the cartons and not even bother to get out the dinner plates. Mom might frown at that, but Kenzie and I think it's fun.

My friends and I have a lot of sleepovers and snuggle together watching scary movies—my neighbors Emma and Sydney have a movie room in her house, so we pop popcorn or bake brownies or chocolate-chip cookies and have our own screening. The last movie we watched was *The Conjuring 2*. We always wind up terrified, but if we're together, we're fine. It's like, safety in numbers. To my friends, the fact that I'm on TV or videos or the movies is no biggie. They might send me a Snapchat from the airport of my face on a magazine cover—"Oh, look! It's you lol"—but that's the most they'll ever really talk about it. It's just what I do; it's not who I am. They'd much rather gossip about clothes or boys or try out new makeup.

I'm homeschooled but I take tests and write papers and usually spend four hours a day during the school year working with my tutor. My favorite subjects are English and math; science not so much. I love a good book, and the last one I read was *Me and Earl and the Dying Girl* by Jesse Andrews. Sad, sad, sad. My favorite books ever were *Freak the Mighty* and *Wonder*—both brought me to tears. I love writing my own stories, and I'll often draw an illustration to go with them. I have a really vivid imagination, so the stories can be kinda out there sometimes, but I love letting my creativity run wild. I'm also a doodle-holic. There isn't a piece of paper around the house that doesn't have one of my scribbles on it. Put a pencil or a pen in my hand and I'll draw—eyes, hearts, lightning bolts, lips, you name it.

I know I'm lucky; I know that "average" teenage girls don't get all the opportunities I've been given. But I also feel on so many levels that I am just a regular kid. My mom yells at me when I'm texting on my phone (probably because I'm tuning her out), and she lost it when I used up all the data on our family phone plan streaming Netflix (I couldn't help it! I was on the last season of *Gossip Girl!*). My little sister hides my things where I can't find them (like in her closet!). We both always try to get out of doing our homework. There are days I look in the mirror and think to myself, *Ugh! My stomach looks bloated,* or, *My thighs are jiggly,* or, *My face is broken out,* or, *My hair looks flat.* On a daily basis, I open my closet and can't find a single thing to wear.

I have the same insecurities that every girl my age has; that doesn't change because I'm in the public eye. In fact, sometimes it makes me even more insecure. I have to worry about a photo of me looking terrible going viral on the internet. Or I might wind up in a weekly's "worst-dressed" spread for a choice I made on the red carpet. If these things happened in school, it would be considered bullying. But because I'm an entertainer, it's part of the job. When you put yourself out there, you make yourself an easy target. People will judge you for whatever reason—they're jealous, they don't like themselves, they're having a bad day. I've learned to not take it personally. If I did, I'd be upset all the time, because there is an awful lot of hating that goes on in this world. Social media is a great thing, but it makes hating on others really easy. The best you can do is ignore it; let it bounce off you. Like Sia sings in "Titanium": "You're bulletproof; nothing to lose, fire away." Surround yourself with people who love you and appreciate you for who you truly are.

I like that my mom has always made it her mission to keep my feet firmly planted on the ground—when I'm not dancing, of course. Anytime something threatens to go to my head—say, being photographed recently for *Vanity Fair* or appearing on the Grammys with Sia—she brings me back down to earth and tells me to go make my bed (just so you know, it was Kenzie's turn to do it today, but she forgot). I've met a few people in Hollywood, and it's clear that fame has gotten to them—they're not gracious or polite; they think they're better than everyone else. In the dance competition world, we learned you're only as good as your last performance—you're top of the pyramid this week, bottom the next. I think that goes for life in general.

You always have to keep working hard and treating others the way you want to be treated. I'll be totally honest here: Sometimes all the things I do in my career feel a little like an out-of-body experience. I'm always going to be me, and I wouldn't want it any other way.

## Pinch-Me Moments

**Over the years, I've had some really amazing—and really crazy—experiences, from winning awards, to walking the red carpet, to meeting celebs face-to-face. Like Justin Bieber!**

**"Chandelier," 2014.** I remember thinking to myself, *I wonder if anyone is gonna see this.* I had no idea it would literally explode and celebs would be tweeting how much it inspired them. Ellen DeGeneres raved, and *Glee* star Naya Rivera tweeted, "Ok my jaw is completely dropped at how good this @Sia 'chandelier' video is." I remember I decided to check the number of views on YouTube and it said more than six million people had watched it—this was in the first few days!

**Kids' Choice Awards, 2012.** I was about nine at the time, and all the girls from *Dance Moms* got to go—this was our first awards show. We were all wearing pink, and I re-member we matched the pink carpet! I had always had a major fangirl crush on Justin Bieber—when people asked me, "What star would you like to dance with?" I would always say him. And then there he was: in this cool camo

T-shirt with that spiky-hair thing going on. If I look at the photos the paparazzi took of all of us with him, my face is utter joy—and maybe shock. He was very gracious and posed with his arm around me.

**Teen Choice Awards, 2013–16.** We've gone every year, first as a cast, and then as individual nominees. I was voted Choice Dancer in 2016, which meant I got to take home the surfboard (which is so cool, and kinda heavy, BTW). I also got to do this cute skit with Cat Deeley where we pretended to be judging hosts Victoria Justice and John Cena on their dancing skills. I used to watch *Victorious* on TV when I was younger, so that was really wild . . .

**People's Choice Awards, 2016.** I was in this category, DailyMail.com's Seriously Popular Award, nominated with Kylie Jenner, Ruby Rose, Cara Delevingne, and Bella Thorne. And I won. That is just insane! My friends were all texting me: "You beat Kylie Jenner? OMG!"

*Ballerina*, **coming out in 2017.** I got to voice a character in this animated movie, which was a lot of fun. I had to go into a sound booth and watch the character on the screen and then get my voice to match her lips. It's called ADR, which stands for *automated dialogue* *replacement* (in case you were wondering!). It was so much fun, and Elle Fanning is starring in it. It takes place in 1884 at the Opera Ballet School, and I play the spoiled mean girl. I can't wait to see how it turns out on-screen!

**The Dizzy Feet Foundation's Celebration of Dance Gala, 2016.** It's *the* dance event of the fall, and I got to perform at it with Travis Wall. I love what Dizzy Feet does: They support dance education programs for kids in low-income areas and provide scholarships so they can take classes. You hear these people talking about how if it weren't for Dizzy Feet, they'd be on the street or selling drugs. It's really powerful and it felt amazing to be a part of it. Dance changed their lives. Also, you see so many celebs come out to support it: This year, they honored Derek and Julianne Hough from *Dancing with the Stars*, so I got to hang with two of my idols.

***Time* magazine's "The 30 Most Influential Teens of 2015."** This was such an honor—and kind of surreal, because that list included entrepreneurs, gold medalists, TV stars, someone who invented a test for the Ebola virus, Kylie and Kendall Jenner, Zendaya, Shawn Mendes, Bethany Mota, Bindi Irwin, Malia Obama, and Silentó—the guy who did "Watch Me (Whip/Nae Nae)." Very, very cool to be included among this group.

**Fashion dolls, 2016.** So when I did the "Broken Dolls" number on *Dance Moms* in 2014, I never actually imagined I would one day *be* a doll! A toy company, Jazwares, created these adorable fashion dolls of me and Kenzie. They're so cute—they come with their little mini dance bags for the studio. The process was actually pretty intense: We took tons of pictures showing our faces from all angles, and the company created these cute little clay prototypes and kept tweaking them till they looked just like us. I love that mine has on character shoes!

**Industry Dance Awards, 2016.** Kenzie presented me with the 2016 Breakthrough Performer Award. She called me "smart, beautiful, and talented" and said I worked really hard. I had no idea about the speech she was giving—so I thanked her for being nice! Then choreographer Mandy Moore surprised me and came up after my acceptance speech to hug me. She said, "I love this little lady so much," which made me blush. It was such a special moment, and I love Mandy so much, too.

## Memories of Maddie

"We met the Zieglers at a meet-and-greet more than five years ago. The show wasn't a phenomenon yet, and my daughter Lilia and Maddie really clicked. Every time they would come to L.A., we would see them, or we would go visit them in Pittsburgh. They would stay with us often; the girls became like sisters, and the Zieglers became our second family. We have so many fun memories, too many to count. Melissa and I call each other 'Sister Wives'! I remember one time, I took Maddie and Lilia to Craig's, which is a neighborhood restaurant. The paparazzi were outside, taking pictures of us going inside—they recognized Maddie from TV. We sat down in a booth, and the girls noticed someone in the seat directly next to ours—it was Kris Jenner and she was FaceTiming one of her daughters, Khloé or Kim or Kourtney. Lilia and Maddie were dying! They tried sneaking over and were huddled in a corner of the booth, trying to spy on her. In Maddie's mind, the Kardashians were the famous ones, not her.

"But that's Maddie. She's the most humble, grounded kid you will ever meet. And she has the cutest sense of humor. We have a whiteboard on my fridge where we write our grocery list: 'Eggs, bread, milk.' One day she writes on the list, 'Zac Efron.' The housekeeper goes shopping and comes home completely perplexed.

"'I couldn't find this,' she says, pointing to the last item. 'What is Zac Efron?' Like it was a spice or a breakfast cereal! We all had a great laugh over it.

"When Maddie leaves, she puts little notes in our cabinets: 'We will miss you! Love you, Lilia! Jack is great!' My sixteen-year-old son is like a big brother to her. We find these little 'Maddie missives' everywhere and they make us smile.

"I have to say, I'm really impressed by her. Having been in Hollywood for thirteen years, you see a lot of young stars that can't handle fame. She's wise beyond her years, and she handles it beautifully and graciously and wisely. She is respectful and appreciative of every opportunity and takes nothing for granted. She's stayed true to her real friends and has never been swayed by the trappings that often come with this life. She loves what she does. She loves dancing, and that comes through; it's pure joy to her. She doesn't want to go to every party or get free stuff or rub elbows with celebrities—she's remarkably modest and polite.

"We tease her, 'We're going to start fining you a quarter for every time you apologize!' It's true—she's always saying, 'Sorry.' She'll ask, 'Can I have some milk with my cereal—I'm sorry.' She never wants to be a burden or a bother.

"I think she gets a lot of her kind heart from her mom. The Buckinghams have gone through some difficult times, and Melissa and the girls have supported us and loved us more than just family friends—it shows the kind of people that they are. Good people are good people, and they are the best kind of people: real, genuine, loving."

—Jane Buckingham, family friend

"So when I first met Maddie I was a little intimidated. I mean, she was the girl from *Dance Moms* . . . hello? We went outside and ate pizza and played a game. She was the most humble girl and we bonded immediately—we were both about eight years old. I consider her my best friend. When she stays in my house, we watch romance movies and cry. I'm proud to say I introduced her to *The Notebook*.

"'What do you mean you've never seen it?' I asked

her. 'You *have* to see it!' So we watched it and sobbed our eyes out. We love to go to Katsuya and just sit around with each other—we make each other laugh. She painted me a painting for two hours and I loved just watching her. We don't talk about dance too much—if she's excited about something like Sia, I'll hear about it, but it doesn't ever really come up. Instead, it's more girl talk. She knows all of my school drama—she's like my sister in that way. I tell her everything.

"I miss her a lot when she's gone. She stayed with us for two weeks and that was amazing. She slept in my room and kept me up all night gabbing. It always goes something like this:

"'All right, good night, Lilia.' Pause. 'Wait! Guess what!' Then we're up for an hour talking about something completely random. I feel like we never run out of things to say to each other. People always ask me what's it like to be friends with Maddie. Well, it's great, because she's one of the best people I've ever met. She's as loyal and down-to-earth as she was before all of this fame happened. In fact, I think it's made her a better person: She doesn't take anything for granted, and she is so grateful and kind to everyone.

"Some of the stuff that has happened to her ... oh my gosh, it's crazy. Melissa gave me and my mom the Maddie and Kenzie dolls before they came out. Dolls! Like little Barbies! Who has a doll of themselves? We would take them and put them in back of the car and send the Zieglers a photo: 'Taking the girls to school!' We'd sit them at the kitchen table: 'Breakfast with the girls.' It was pretty hilarious.

"Since Maddie has moved out to L.A. part-time I've gotten to see her more. But with the Sia tour, it's been hard. She's all over the country and so, so busy. We text, we FaceTime, we Snapchat. There isn't a day that goes by that we don't. I went to see her perform at the Hollywood Bowl. When she first appeared onstage, my mom and I were dying: 'It's our little Maddie!' We had such a feeling of pride. I told her, 'I want to make you a giant sign with your face on it and hold it up from the audience.' She was like, 'Don't! It'll creep me out! I don't want to look out there and see *me*!'

"What I love most about Maddie is her heart. The first time she came to stay with us, I was going through kind of a hard time. We went to dinner, and she leaned across the table and said, 'If you ever need anyone to talk to, I'm here.' She meant it. She's someone who is fiercely loyal. And she scream-sings at me whenever I am freaking out. She is so talented at everything—acting, dancing... but not singing. Not at all. So we will make these crazy videos whenever I'm stressed out before a test. She embraces the fact that she can't sing and really goes for it—you have to hold your ears. We have our greatest hits: 'In the Name of Love' by Martin Garrix and 'Higher' by Rihanna. She can really rap, and you don't need to be in tune for that. Actually, I want to rap-battle her! I think we need to put that on our to-do list..." —Lilia Buckingham, Maddie's BFF

## *Dear Maddie*

**I feel like I'm always eating junk. I'm so busy—what can I eat on the run?**

I'm big on protein bars—there is always an assortment in my bag along with a banana and a big bottle of water. They're my go-to "on the go" snacks. If I have more time, I might pack a small container of blueberries or chopped strawberries and some granola. I know a lot of people eat Greek yogurt on the run. It's super healthy and full of protein, but I've never liked it very much. Unless it's key lime flavor—that one I love. If I'm at dance and I need to grab dinner, my mom will bring me a grilled chicken breast and some broccoli. You can also do a roll-up of turkey with some cheese. The point is to prepare ahead of time, so you're not hitting the vending machine for candy or the drive-thru for a double cheeseburger and fries. If you stock up your home with healthy snacks, you'll be able to eat on the run much healthier.

**I think this girl in my studio is a terrible dancer, and she just got the lead in our studio showcase. I don't understand! I'm so much better than her, and it makes me mad.**

The best dancers don't always get the biggest parts. That's just how it goes. You may be technically a better dancer than she is, but maybe she is more "suited" to the part—like maybe she's a good actor, or has a great work ethic, or she's simply the right height or fits the costume better. Try not to take it personally and keep working hard—it won't go unnoticed. Sometimes you don't know what a choreographer or teacher is looking for. This time, whatever it was, she had it. There will be other opportunities for you to shine.

**I messed up big-time. We were doing a jazz group dance at a competition, and I totally blanked and forgot the steps. I ruined the dance for everyone and we lost. Now I'm worried my team is going to hate me!**

If you're a team, they won't blame or hate you. It happens to everyone. I've forgotten my steps; every single girl on my team has. Don't feel guilty, and don't assume that you're the reason for losing; other people may have messed up, too. So you didn't win? So what? Next time you'll do better—think of this as a chance to learn from your mistakes. Why did you forget the steps? Did you practice enough? Get enough sleep the night before? Did you get nervous onstage? Figure it out so you can fix it, then move on.

 *Today Is a Beautiful Day to . . .*

* **Do something sporty**—even if it's from the sidelines. I would never turn down going to a Pittsburgh Pirates game with my girls!

* **Say thank you.** People need to hear it. On Mother's Day, I posted "Thank you for everything you do!" on my Insta account and my mom got all mushy. But you don't need a holiday to show your appreciation. Today, pick one person who does something for you and tell them you're grateful. Even the nice lady who makes your smoothie at the juice store!

* **Make a dessert date with a friend.** Personally, my fave one involves creating, not just eating—I go to Duff's Cakemix in L.A. and decorate cakes. Kalani and I are experts! But it's also a lot of fun to just drive to the local Dairy Queen for a sweet treat or bake brownies in your kitchen.

· Chapter Five ·

# SIA'S MINI-ME

The day I saw the tweet I thought it was a joke. Sia Furler, this huge pop star from Australia, reached out to me—*me!*—and asked if I wanted to be in her next video. It literally said, "Hey Maddie, you want to be in my next video? Melissa, my people are trying to get in touch . . ."

I held it up to show my mom: "I don't believe this. I mean, it can't be real, right?"

But it *was* real: Sia had seen me on *Dance Moms* and was a fan of the show and specifically my dancing. We got in touch with her and I flew out to L.A. two weeks later. I had no idea what to expect—I was eleven at the time, and I'd never done anything like this before. I had heard her song "Chandelier," and I assumed I'd be one of several background dancers. I also thought that swinging from a chandelier might be involved (which kind of sounded fun). When I got to the rehearsal space, I was shocked that no one else was there to learn the choreography. "You mean it's just me?" I asked. "No one else is dancing?" I looked at the set, a long dark hallway and an abandoned apartment: "Can someone go in there with me?" I was a little creeped out. What did I get myself into? I mean, where was the chandelier? Where were the people? Why were the rugs all stained and ripped?

Then the choreographer, Ryan Heffington (who is an absolute genius!), went through the moves and talked me through what he and Sia were envisioning. He used words like *haunted* and *hoarders*. Hmmm . . . It felt strange to be doing something that didn't involve pointed toes and perfect legs. They actually *wanted* me to look crazy and off-balance. And the faces I had to make? Well, they were freaky. One was called "hissing cat." At first, I worried I'd look weird and people would laugh. But Ryan encouraged me to let go and get out of my head. I wasn't Maddie; I was playing a character, and this character kicked her feet and pulled her hair and beat her fists and made crazy eyes. The dancing had to feel crazy as well—Ryan mentioned "manic." He told me this was "my" world and I was stuck here, trapped, but it was also familiar to me—I knew every corner, every inch. I cannot thank Ryan enough for introducing me to the coolest style of dance—he's helped me grow like no one else. Ryan's assistant choreographer, Denna Thomsen, was also amazing—I look up to her so much.

They had planned on rehearsing for four days, but I learned the dance in just a few hours. Then Sia came into the rehearsal space to watch. She was so funny—a real *Dance Moms* fangirl. She screamed when she saw me and said, "I can't believe you're here and I'm hugging you!" I wasn't even sure it was her at first—I'd never seen her face in any recent photos. People think she covers her face all the time, but that's only when she's in public. When she's just hanging out, there is no wig or paper bag—just her sweet, smiley face. From that first moment when we met, we felt an instant connection—like we'd known each other all our lives. I can't explain it—we just get each other. And when I showed her the dance, she cried—so I knew I had done something right. A few weeks later she said, "You want to do my next two videos with me?" It was the beginning of an amazing collaboration and friendship.

Now I'm totally comfortable making the crazy faces! You ask me to roll my eyes, grit my teeth, stick out my tongue—not a prob! On *Ellen*, when I did "Elastic Heart," I didn't move my legs at all (I was standing in a big white box). There were all these little girls behind me in the Sia wigs, tucked into white boxes, so all you could see were their heads lip-synching along. Ellen must have been like, "Whoa, what is this?" But she and Sia are pals and she's had us on a lot of times and loves Sia. She knows she's never going to bring on something boring! In this case, it was all about the crazy face. Same with the "Big Girls Cry" video—it's shot from the waist up (except for the few seconds when I'm hanging there kicking in the air), with me pushing and pulling my cheeks, lips, and eyes and staring at the camera.

I've gotten really good at not being self-conscious about it. It's kind of a funny thing to put on a résumé ("does good crazy face"), but it's acting, because there's a lot of emotion that's behind those faces. It's telling a story: We choreograph my face. It isn't just random or silly. Sia and Ryan always make sure I am comfortable with all the choreography and they always value my input.

# Wigging Out

**People are always asking me about the wigs I wear when I work with Sia. So here are some fun facts...**

**The one I wore on the Grammys' red carpet is different from the one in the videos.** It's thicker—I want to say "pouffier." My hairstylist Tonya actually had to crimp it with an iron and spray it with an entire can of hair spray. As big as mine was, Sia's was bigger... and heavier... and so thick she couldn't see through it. I had to literally guide her around the red carpet. I was like her seeing-eye dog for the night!

**It takes a gazillion pins to keep it in place.** I'm always worried it's going to fall off, so we go a little crazy securing it. First we braid my hair; then we wrap those braids and pin them on top of my head. Then I put on a wig cap. The wig gets pinned into the cap and the "nest" of braids we've created under it to anchor it all. Last count, I think we used 150 pins, but I might be off by a dozen or so. But if I flipped and it fell off, that would be awful.

**It's not too itchy,** but it does get a little hot when I'm dancing. Like I'm wearing a helmet or shrink-wrap on my head.

**Under her wig,** Sia is beautiful inside and out. She doesn't want people to see her face because she doesn't want to be famous. When we hang, we hang up the wigs. I'm one of the few people who knows what she looks like!

"Chandelier" definitely changed my life—it made me more than just the girl from *Dance Moms*. It opened a lot of doors and opportunities for me. Honestly, the attention all came as a shock—I thought I was making a little video. I had no idea it would be this big. More than a billion people (I said a billion, not a million!) saw it, and it's something like the seventeenth-most viewed video ever. *Rolling Stone* named it the top video of 2014.

Suddenly I was doing interviews on national news shows and accompanying Sia on the red carpet. When we went to the Grammys, we dressed in twin tuxedos and the paparazzi were screaming, "Sia, take off your wig! Maddie, do a somersault!" Like I would do that in public? This year, I toured twenty-six cities with her on the Nostalgic for the Present tour. I performed on *Ellen*, the Grammys, *Saturday Night Live*, and *Jimmy Kimmel Live* (where I taught him and Guillermo "how to fly through the night and swing"). I'm told the wig and nude leotard were one of the most popular Halloween costumes in 2014—people actually went trick-or-treating dressed like me. "Chandelier" was nominated for four Grammys, and I got to be there to celebrate with Sia and perform it live with Kristen Wiig (who, for not being a dancer, was a really great dancer!). For the record, it was a total pinch-me moment. I looked out at the audience, and there were Kim and Kanye watching me. I wanted to freak out, but I kept my cool and behaved like a professional.

Backstage, I bumped into Gwen Stefani. "Oh, hey! You're amazing," she told me. I looked around: *You talkin' to me?* People used to stop me on the street and say, "You're that girl from *Dance Moms*." Virtually overnight it became, "You're that girl from the 'Chandelier' video."

After "Chandelier," we did videos for "Elastic Heart," "Big Girls Cry," "Cheap Thrills," and "The Greatest." With each one, I feel like I stretched myself a little more—when I performed "Alive" on *Ellen*, I had to punch my fist through a pane of glass. They're all very physically demanding. I don't think I've ever been as covered in dirt as I was for "Elastic Heart"— literally filthy. When I went home and took a shower after shooting, the water looked like mud. I'm kind of a neat freak, so after every rehearsal in the cage, I'd change my clothes and use wipes to try and clean myself up, but it didn't help. After a while I just gave up. The more I tried to stay clean, the more they kept covering me in black smudges. Shia LaBeouf, my costar in the video, didn't seem to mind, but then again, he's a guy. Guys don't mind being messy.

Sia knows some of the emotions I have to portray in her videos are really intense, and she'll say, "If it's too much for you, you have to say, 'I can't handle it.'" But I'm not afraid to go for it—she's helped me be a braver actor. I think of her as a big sister, a second mom, and my best friend; she's family. I told my mom last week I wanted to move in and live with her in L.A. (I was only half-kidding). Sia always tells me, "If you didn't have such a great family, I'd adopt you." She gives me great advice. She told me that when she was younger and she was a songwriter, she got burnt out because she worked constantly. She always warns me that if all you do is work, you wind up hating something you once loved. "Be a kid," she always tells me. "You work harder than any adult I know!"

Before I met her, I would say yes a lot to things I didn't want to do because I thought I had to—I didn't want to disappoint anyone. I'd be overwhelmed by the amount of work I had on my plate. But now, if I need a day off, I say so. Sia always tells me you have to take time off, step back, and appreciate the moment. You have to cherish the little things. When I'm with her, I laugh a lot, and anything I'm worrying about just melts away. She always tells me, "Stay humble, be grateful," and I think that's the best advice. She's been through some bad times and seen a lot. Instead of letting that hold her back or weigh her down, it's lifted her up and made her wiser. She doesn't take a single thing for granted, and she reminds me that life is what you make of it—so you better make it the best ride you can.

## Five Things I Love, Love, Love About Sia

*1*    Her crazy laugh. It's impossible for me to imitate, but it's kind of like, "Huh-HAH!" She also giggles a lot.

*2*    Going to movies and out for sushi with her. She wrote the music for *Zootopia* and we went to see it together. When we go out, people recognize me and not her, because she's not wearing the wig. Someone even asked me, "Is this your mom?"

*3*    Being part of her family—she took me to a wedding recently with her and her hubby in Philly. People call me her "muse" or her "protégé," but she calls me her BFF.

*4*    Her amazing doggies, Cereal, Pantera, and Lickey. They are like my family, too.

*5*    She's so normal. Even though she's this humungous superstar, she's the most regular person you'll ever meet. She's the opposite of a diva!

*On Tour With Sia*

October 15, 2016: As I'm writing this, we have thirteen more concerts left to go on the tour—which means we're halfway through. I can't even think about that, because it makes me so sad. I am loving every minute of this experience, and I don't want it to ever end. So I won't keep track of how many cities we already logged or how many more we have to go. I'm just trying to live in the moment and pretend there's no end date.

We did the West Coast lap of the tour and now we're heading east—Boston; Washington, DC; and New York; and all over Canada as well. Then we head south to Florida, Georgia, New Orleans, and Texas. We travel everywhere on the bus, which is more like a home on wheels. It's huge and outfitted with everything you can think of, from TVs, fridges, and couches to bunk beds. I'm on the top bunk and my mom sleeps on the bottom—we're tour buddies, and I'd be a lot more homesick if she wasn't here with me. She puts her arms up sometimes because she's afraid I'll fall out of the top bunk! I have my own dressing room at each venue, but I never use it—I like to hang with the dancers. Instead, my mom camps out in there and makes it her own.

We've literally been on the road for the past fifteen hours, driving from Chicago to Boston, and I can't say I'm bored. Sia surprised me with a professional massage yesterday, and that was an amazing treat (my legs and feet get really sore from all the dancing). I'm rewatching *Gossip Girl* on Netflix with Tonya (my tour BFF and hair/makeup stylist). I also slept really late this morning—till about eleven thirty. I woke up and it was already lunchtime. You can't blame me: We didn't get to bed till 3 a.m. because the concert doesn't end till midnight, and then we have to pack everything up. So yeah, I needed to catch up on my sleep. I feel like everyone on this tour is family—even Tonya's dog, who makes the smelliest farts and stinks up the bus, lol! Occasionally, we have a day off to go shopping or go out to eat as a group, but mostly we just go from venue to venue, city to city, performing for the fans.

The stadium crowds are ginormous—you look out, and it's a sea of faces, thousands and thousands of them. I always get nervous, which I know sounds crazy, because I should be used to doing the shows now. But it's a total rush. We do sixteen numbers total, and I dance in six or seven of them. Stephanie Mincone is like my twin; she does the other half of the dances in the same wigs and nude leotard, because it's just too much for one person to do. We look so much alike, people actually think it's me up there for the whole concert. Wanna tell us apart? She's a little more muscular than I am, and I'm a little taller. And she's the one who gets to wear the panda head, FYI, in "Titanium." Steph's become one of my best friends and we got so close on tour; she's literally my other half. We think the same, we talk the same, and I love her so much—she's my favorite person. I used to go to her hotel room and watch *RuPaul's Drag Race* with her—the boys on tour, Nick and Wyatt, got us hooked on it. All four of us would watch it in the dressing room, and Floris, the other male dancer, would say, "Can we *please* watch something else?" Wyatt and I were duo buddies; he brought his Wii on the bus and we played Mario Kart and the boys would always beat me. Nick was the first male dancer they cast in the show and he made sure we were on time because he was "the responsible one." Floris was a big brother to me—he was always asking me, "Did you eat? Did you drink?" before a show. He was always looking out for me.

When the tour came to an end, it was so hard for us to say goodbye; we were bawling. I kept saying, "I can't believe we're all leaving each other." We were a tight-knit little family. But the good news is we'll be doing it again one day—Sia has promised this isn't the end. She said we will always be her family.

The first song I dance to is "Alive," and the audience screams when I come out. Sia is singing, and these dancers in white ruffled costumes make up the layers of her skirt. Suddenly, they back off and it's my big reveal. Then it's just me and Sia onstage, and it's real and surreal at the same time.

Celebs sometimes surprise us and come meet us backstage. I don't really get starstruck very often, but Jennifer Aniston came the other day and I was so excited to meet her. She's one of my acting idols, and she said she was super inspired by the show. We talked for a while and she is so sweet and genuine and I look up to her a lot.

I think I was walking on air that night when I climbed back on the bus. Most of the time I'm so tired, my head hits the pillow and I'm out like a light. It's like you're so pumped up, so full of energy and anticipation . . . and then the show ends and your battery runs out. I need to recharge! But onstage, there's no feeling like it in the world.

Sia says, "This is where you were meant to be," and I know she's right.

I spent my fourteenth birthday on the tour. We were in San Francisco at the time, and Sia surprised me by taking our whole gang to a bakery to decorate cakes. When we were done, we all went out for sushi—which is my favorite food. She knows me so well! Tonya also gave me the best gift that night: She held up her phone, and on it was a video from Zac Efron wishing me a happy birthday! I don't know how she did it, but she did. I was crying, I was so excited. Cake, sushi, Zac . . . what more could a girl ask for?

## Memories of Maddie

"I first met Maddie at one of our rehearsals for Sia back in February of 2016. We jumped right into work and learning choreography. I was blown away by her work ethic and talent, but also by how sweet and humble she was. Not to mention, her professionalism and maturity are admirable. When we first met, we were both the same height, and now she's at least three inches taller than me! She's my big little sister.

"Maddie and I have shared endless laughs in our times spent together on the Nostalgic for the Present tour. We always joke around and say that we're twins, because it's scary how similar our personalities and sense of humors are. One of my favorite memories with Maddie has to be when we had a slumber party in my hotel room in Las Vegas. The night consisted of multiple episodes of *Project Runway*, jumping on the bed, room service, and good ol' girl talk. That same night, we had also given each other blindfolded makeovers—I'm sure you could imagine how those turned out. While on tour we binge-watched *RuPaul's Drag Race* and finished three seasons. It became a preshow ritual. Any time I spend with Maddie is my favorite time and is always filled with laughs and love.

"Spending so much time with Maddie the past couple months, I feel like I've really gotten to learn a lot about her and grow a true sisterly bond with her. She's one of the most caring and genuine people I've ever met. She's always concerned with other people's well-being and happiness. I don't think I've seen her interact with someone and not bring joy to the conversation or a smile to their face. She's a total goof with a heart of pure gold. She's humble and down-to-earth. There's not many other ways to put it, other than that she is an extremely special girl. Even though I'm six years older than her, I'm so inspired by her, and she's taught me more than she knows."

—Stephanie Mincone, dancer, Sia's Nostalgic for the Present tour (and Maddie's "twin")

*Dear Maddie*

**My mom and dad just told me they're getting a divorce. I'm really freaking out—I feel like we won't be a family anymore and it's all my fault.**

First of all, it's not your fault. Your parents don't think that and you shouldn't either. Their relationship just isn't working the way it was and they don't want to be unhappy. When my mom and dad divorced, I was upset at first. But I can truly tell you it's not the end of the world. I thought it would be, but then I realized it was way better, because now I didn't have to worry about them fighting or being in a horrible mood. They will always be a part of your life and always love you, even if they're not together. And for me, the good news was I got two Christmases! Be really honest with your parents about what you're feeling—tell them if you're sad or freaking out. They will help you through this like mine did. And just know that you're not alone—tons of kids have divorced moms and dads, and we all felt like you did when we first found out. It gets better, I promise.

**My friend asked me to do her homework for her—she's really busy with dance class and doesn't have time. I feel like it's cheating, but if I don't do it, I'm worried she won't like me anymore.**

It *is* cheating. And you're not doing her any favors. She'll never learn unless she does her assignments on her own. My advice would be to tell her you will sit with her and help her with her homework if she doesn't understand it, but you're not going to give her the answers. Explain that you care about her, and helping her cheat is not being a good friend. If she's your friend, she'll understand. If she doesn't like you anymore, then she was probably using you all along and you're better off without her.

**Do you ever get freaked out that you're famous—like when someone asks you for your autograph? Do you ever want to cover your face like Sia?**

Well, sometimes it's a little overwhelming, I'll be honest with you. Like when I'm just trying to walk around and be with friends and someone runs up to me and sticks their camera in my face and says, "Take a picture with me!" Sometimes people are rude and don't even say hi, they just demand a selfie! But for the most part, fans are really sweet and polite and I don't mind. I wouldn't be here if it wasn't for everyone out there supporting me and following me. I realize that I chose this life and this career, and that's kind of all part of it. I'm not gonna complain—I owe my fans so much.

$\mathcal{M}$y favs.

*K*risten was
so much fun!!

*J*immy Kimmel
performance!

*M*e and Steph in New Orleans! We took so many pics that day!

*R*ehearsal for *DWTS* with Allison and Ryan! Love them both.

*M*y fav pic of us! She's so gorgeous.

*T*he night I put rainbow tears on Tonya!

The most amazing
Travis Wall.

The beautiful Bella
and me at the Zac
Posen show!

*D*inner with Kate Moss and her daughter in England.

*K*aty Perry at the VMAs!

*M*e and JLo matching in our silver, lol.

*T*ough day at work.

*T*he time I met the nicest woman, Gwen!

*O*ne of the best days ever! Ahhh can't believe I won a surfboard.

*L*ove the Houghs!

*G*reat night at the Dizzy Feet Gala.

*M*et superstar
Laurie Hernandez at CBS!

*M*y SYTYCD family. Such an amazing group of people.

*W*ith the beautiful Naomi Watts while we were filming *The Book of Henry*!

*T*eaching my little bro Jacob Tremblay how to do a split :)

Millie Bobby Brown and me at the Wizarding World of Harry Potter.

One of our traditions before every show.

Greatest selfie ever, Mo

$\mathcal{I}$ had such an amazing time touring with Sia in 2016.

$\mathcal{S}$ome of the best times of my life!

# Today Is a Beautiful Day to . . .

* **Get inspired.** Research and read about someone who you think is a great role model—a person in history, a celeb, an icon, etc. Make a list of three important things they say/believe that you can use to make your own life greater. Sia is obviously someone I really look up to, but I also am inspired by celebs with great style—like Kendall Jenner, Ariana Grande, Selena. Those girls always look good!

* **Chill.** Take a yoga class; go for some pampering at a mani/pedi place; take a few deep breaths and let the tension drain away. Here's another funny way to relax: Yawn! Someone told me that it actually lifts your mood and helps you think clearer. Just cover your mouth when you do—my mom always says it's not polite to yawn in someone's face!

* **Whip up some jewelry.** This was something Kenzie and I used to love to do, especially with beads or rainbow-colored rubber bands. I love finding jewelry how-tos on YouTube that look fun to make. Stock up

on supplies like wire, beads, clasps, etc. at a craft store. That way, the next time you're twiddling your thumbs and complaining you have nothing to do, you'll be ready. An added bonus (besides fighting off boredom): You'll have an instant new accessory to show for it!

· *Chapter Six* ·

# SO I THINK
# I CAN JUDGE

After all those years of being judged at dance competitions—some where they actually make you stand up there and smile while they pick apart every single thing you did wrong—the idea of being a judge on *So You Think You Can Dance: The Next Generation* sounded so cool. But the other judges? Well, they're huge. Legends, to be exact. Paula Abdul is tiny, but she has had this big career as a singer, dancer, actress, and choreographer (she actually choreographed Janet Jackson's videos, which is *crazy*!). I'm not sure there's anything the woman *hasn't* done. I became really close to her because she and I were the girls of the group. She's so silly and fun, and we always agreed when it came to judging. I call Nigel Lythgoe "Papa Nigel"—he's been a dancer, choreographer, director, and producer and judged a gazillion shows. Everyone in the dance world knows his name and he's practically royalty. And Jason Derulo—well, he's sold millions of singles including some of my faves, "Wiggle" and "Talk Dirty." He's the coolest person on the planet, period.

Then there's me. I'm someone closer to the age of the competitors and just starting out in my career. My résumé is nowhere near as long as my fellow judges', and I've grown up watching the show and looking up to the dancers my whole life. When they first approached me I was in shock—I thought they wanted me for a guest judge spot, a onetime thing. "You want me to be on the show the whole time?" I gasped. "That's insane." I felt a little out of my league the first day I took my seat with the other judges. But the self-doubt quickly melted away as soon as I realized I did have a lot to bring to the table (literally, lol!). The first few shows I was nervous, so my comments were a little basic: "You guys did a great job!" But as we got further along, I definitely felt more confident speaking in front of a live audience. I wanted to give each dancer something they could take away with them to help them improve; I watched carefully and gave them a few pointers that would create a stronger performance.

The only problem is the timer! There's a screen in front of each of the judges at the table that shows how many minutes and seconds we all have left to speak. It's supposed to be about four minutes total between the four of us, but Nigel likes to talk *a lot*. But that's because he's so experienced and knows everything about every dance in the world! I love him. So sometimes it will get to my turn and I literally have two seconds to share my thoughts. If that's the case, the most I can get out is, "Wow!" and an enthusiastic thumbs-up before we have to cut to commercial. Then I feel bad, because I think of a million things I wish I could have said and didn't. But that's live TV for you: If we go over our minutes too often, the show will run late—which is a big no-no. Sometimes on commercial breaks, the producers will remind us, "Keep the comments brief." I like when I get to go first—then I can talk and talk and Nigel is watching his clock waiting for me to wrap it up.

For the 250th episode, I got to partner with Travis Wall in a dance he choreographed specifically for the show. All those weeks I was sitting in the judge's chair, itching to get up there onstage and dance. I was so jealous of the kids dancing. Finally, I had my chance, and with Travis, whom I really admire and love working with. No pressure: just a really huge night in the show's history. Nigel was funny. He told me, "Our first episode was in 2005—were you around then?" We did some quick calculating and I realized I was three years old at the time. Travis was on Season 2 when he was eighteen, and he danced on Broadway when he was twelve. I feel like we have a lot in common—he's always had this passion and drive and it's a lot like mine. He's an amazing mentor for me. I don't have words to describe what a genius he is—his storytelling is just incredible. You literally feel like you can do anything, be anything, because he gives you that freedom as an artist.

We learned our dance in four hours. Travis is very spontaneous; he choreographs on the spot, so you have to really keep up with how fast his mind and his feet work. It was a contemporary dance to the song "Cage of Bones" by Son Lux—a battle between the two of us, light vs. darkness. There were times when his foot was an inch from my face and moments where I was pulling him and dropping him. The lifts were crazy advanced—you really have to trust someone a lot to let them throw you around over their head like that. We were both black and blue and sore after the rehearsal. His back was spasming; I broke blood vessels and had a huge bruise on my knee. We definitely beat each other up. But it was so worth it—such an unforgettable moment, and an incredible experience to work with him again. Our first time dancing together was at the Disneyland sixtieth anniversary dancing to "Part of Your World" from *The Little Mermaid*. This was like the polar opposite of that: dark, fierce, and kind of tribal/warrior. I owe Travis a huge thank-you for making my dreams come true.

I'll also let you in on a little secret: Cat Deeley, the host, says at one point in the show: "Okay, Maddie, you've got two minutes to change for your dance . . . go, go, go!" Well, that didn't actually happen. It couldn't, because the makeup and costume were so time-consuming to get on. Travis and I actually pre-taped the dance earlier. So everyone watching at home might have thought I was a quick-change artist, but I was actually just hiding out backstage for a few minutes. The magic of TV!

## *Partnering with Maddie*

"It's great to work with somebody so very talented and passionate about everything they do. We are watching a true star being born. Maddie's talents will go beyond her younger years; she is taking her exposure in the dance field and launching it into all aspects of the entertainment world. She has the power to be unstoppable.

"She is so easy to work with. At this point in our relationship, she trusts me. I was tossing her around, throwing her up and down, and testing both of our limits. She was completely open to any idea I had, which was so great! Maddie is also a perfectionist and can sometimes get down on herself if she doesn't pick up on something quickly. However, as long as she trusts herself, she maintains that quality of excellence we have come to know as Maddie Ziegler.

"She brings individuality to each dance. She's had so much training and exposure across so many different platforms that she kind of moves from a unique place that is her own. Keeping your identity when you dance while also being given choreography is such a difficult task for most dancers. It's impressive she can achieve that at such a young age."—Travis Wall

Especially after this experience with Travis, I always wanted to jump in with the contestants who get to work with these amazing choreographers and all-stars on the show. My favorite part of every week is getting to go into the dance studio and watch them figuring it all out. I see them breaking it down and then piecing it all together. That's usually on a Thursday; then they have Friday and the weekend to perfect it. What the audiences see onstage can be very different from what I watched on a Thursday morning. Most of the time, it's so much better with a few days' practice. I see the kids struggling in the studio, and that's so easy for me to relate to. Each dance is a process to get not just the steps and the technique right, but to connect with the story the choreographer is trying to tell. It's a mind/body game. I love that the show pushes dancers out of their comfort zones—a ballroom dancer may be asked to do a hip-hop routine, and a tap dancer may be challenged to do a lyrical duet. We keep telling the contestants that as a pro, you should be able to go across each of the different styles and disciplines with confidence. Nothing should throw you. I see each of them growing so much, stretching beyond what they ever thought they were capable of doing. There is no "no" on *So You Think You Can Dance*; you try something new even if it scares you. Every time a contestant has said "I can't," they prove themselves wrong and blow us away. I'm so proud of them!

The kids on the show have surprised me and so have the weekly eliminations. I'm shocked sometimes by America's choices, and which competitors wind up in the bottom two. When Jake Monreal and Jordan Wandick were in that bottom position, Paula and I were literally freaking out because we couldn't understand why they were standing there. We kept shaking our heads in disbelief that one of them (it turned out to be Jake) was going home—it was heartbreaking! The worst part is after each elimination, we all go up onstage to say goodbye. There are so many tears and hugs. I find myself saying the same thing each time: "Please don't let this stop you from dancing! You're amazing, and you're going to do great things. I can't wait to see where the future takes you." I mean every word. What they didn't warn me when I took this job is how close I would get to the contestants, how emotionally tied I would feel to them. I was a nervous wreck waiting for the results—I held my breath along with them. I know there can be only one winner, but it's awful to see so many disappointed faces along the way.

As much as it hurts to say goodbye, I've loved every minute of being on the show. I know I'm not a legend yet, but sitting among legends—and helping create new ones—is pretty awesome.

*Dear Maddie*

**My mom thinks she's a teenager! She wants to wear clothes that are way too young for her, and she tries to act "cool." Help—I'm mortified!**

My mom is really good at embarrassing me, too. Her hair, her fake nails (news flash: She just got them off and says they're gone for good! Phew!), the stuff she'll say out loud *very* loudly . . . but I try to cut her some slack because she does so much for me all the time. She drives me everywhere, organizes my life, and when we have a day off she'll treat me to a spa day or take me shopping. I totally relate to what you're saying, but maybe there's a nice, gentle way to tell her how you feel? Otherwise, I say just love her for who she is because she loves you for who you are. I know I embarrass my mom sometimes, too. That's what mothers and daughters do.

**OMG, I really want to be on TV! How can I get on a reality show like you did?**

Well, here's the funny thing: We actually didn't know we were going to be on a reality show. Honestly, I don't think I even knew what a reality show was. When I was cast, my mom's friend pitched the idea to Lifetime and it was supposed to be a documentary for a few weeks following a group of dancers and their moms. We sent in a bunch of dance videos and that was like an audition. From there, things kind of took off. The question I would ask you is this: Why do you want to be on TV so bad? Is it because you want to be famous and have people recognize you, or because you love acting or performing and want to share your talent with a big audience? If your reason is that last part, then you can train, go on auditions, even get an agent. You need to get your family on board, because it can be expensive and time-consuming—you'll need a résumé, headshots, maybe even a film reel to show people. And of course there's coaching, lessons, traveling to auditions . . . I guess what I'm trying to say is that you should follow your dreams but know that nothing happens overnight, especially not a TV show. It will take a lot of work, and there's never any guarantee. You can only do your very best and seek out people who can give you good advice and guidance. In the meantime, if you want screen time, why not make some videos and post them (just get your parents' permission first) online? It will help you get comfortable on camera.

**Do you ever get nervous? I have really bad stage fright—
what should I do?**

I get nervous all the time. I'm a perfectionist and I want
things to go great, so minutes before a big show or performance, my head goes to that "What if?" place. What if I
mess up? What if I forget? I had to perform recently at the
Hollywood Bowl with Sia in front of a huge crowd, and I was
really nervous because I had never danced in front of so
many people. I literally thought, *I'm going to pee my pants!*
Then I got out there, and I forgot about the nerves. I got
through it and you can, too. I think there are a lot of ways to
conquer your fear. First of all, remind yourself how hard you
practiced—you've got this! Don't think about what could go
wrong; instead think of what could go right: You'll do a great
job and the audience will love it. Finally, keep things in perspective: It's not the end of the world if you forget a step or
mess up a lyric. These things happen to everyone. Tell yourself you will go out there and do your very best, and that's
all anyone could ever ask of you. That audience wants you
to wow them—they're rooting for you. With so many people
on your side, there's really no reason to worry, is there?

## Today Is a Beautiful Day to . . .

✳ **Make funny faces in the mirror.** A great stress buster! It reminds you not to take yourself too seriously.

✳ **Watch videos or look at photos of a recent vacation.** It's a fun way to relive those memories and take you back to your "happy place." Mackenzie shot all these videos of us splashing in the pool in Aruba and posted them on her YouTube channel. I see us in the hot tub and on the lazy river and I can actually feel the sun on my face . . . *Ahhh!*

✳ **Pat yourself on the back.** Celebrate something you've accomplished this week—you got an A on your Spanish quiz! You rocked your dance recital! You cleaned your room! Go on, brag a little! Right now, I'm proud of Mackenzie and myself for being nominated as one of TigerBeat.com's 19 Under 19. We're in the same category as some amazing entertainers, and it feels really good to be recognized for doing what we love.

· Chapter Seven ·

# DRAMA QUEEN

*N*igel recently pointed to Kathryn McCormick, one of the all-stars on *The Next Generation*, and said, "The best dancers are the best actors." It's true. When Kathryn dances, her eyes are a window into the soul of her character. Her face conveys every single emotion: fear, pain, joy. So I guess all those years when teachers and judges told me I was good at using my face when I danced, I was really acting. When I was approached to do some roles on TV shows, it seemed like a good idea. I've always wanted to be considered more than a dancer. The first thing I did was a small role on the Lifetime series *Drop Dead Diva*—I was just nine at the time, and I got to play Young Deb. My character was a dancer practicing for nationals, getting really frustrated because she can't get the moves right. My mom/coach is yelling at me, telling me to focus, and I'm yelling back: "I can't!" I do the dance and fall flat on my face, then run off the stage crying. It was the first time I had a script to memorize, but the role was kind of tailor-made for me and easy to relate to—though my mom would never be that mean or critical! She'd be like, "Looks great! Love it!"

I did some more guest spots that were really fun. I played Shelby on *Austin & Ally* on the Disney Channel. My character is this girl who lives in the shadow of her sister Violet, who's an amazing violin player. Austin and Ally make a bet: Who can teach Shelby to play the violin first? But along the way, they figure out that Shelby is actually a much better dancer than a violin player (ya think?). She has this amazing hidden talent (which is why the episode was called "Homework and Hidden Talents"—get it?). In the end, I got to dance with Ross Lynch (who is super cute, by the way, and can do a double pirouette and a time step—who knew?). The song we danced to was called "I'm Finally Me." The whole cast was so nice—they made it easy. But I discovered there's a huge difference between acting onstage and acting on screen. The camera zooms in and captures every movement, every expression—and reactions look much bigger. If you don't want to look like a cartoon, you have to dial it down and be more natural. You're not trying to sell it to the back row. I also love that if you mess up or flub your line, you can always retake. That's something that never happens when you're performing a live dance. If you mess up, you mess up—you don't get a do-over. It's really freeing, because you can try things different ways and see which works best.

On Nickelodeon's *Nicky, Ricky, Dicky & Dawn* I got to play the mean girl for once—a snobby ballerina who wants Dawn's brothers to be her partners in dance class. Kenzie actually did an episode, too; then we did one together, playing sisters. My character's name was Eiffel—as in the tower. Dawn tells me I have to "pas de deux" the dance by myself but I give it to her right back: I tell her the fact that I've been in not one but two toilet paper commercials makes me better than everyone else. I loved doing comedy—and getting to act with a little attitude! Audiences never see that side of me because I would never act mean to someone in the studio or out. But Eiffel is a little evil; at the very least, self-obsessed. I've met my share of mean girls over the years, so I just channeled them.

One of the most exciting acting jobs for me was *Pretty Little Liars*. I'm a huge *PLL* fan—I never miss an episode— and when they asked me to do an opening scene I flipped out. Are you kidding? Do you want me to come to the set, now? I can Uber and be there in five! In the scene, I'm dancing around a creepy room in a white nightgown. If you follow the show, it's supposedly a room inside Radley, the mental institution (double creepy) and I'm a figment of Spencer's tortured mind, her nightmare come to life. I got to do the scene with Troian Bellisario, and she was so humble and inspiring! Travis Wall choreographed it and it was really dark and haunted. There wasn't any music, just chimes, whistles, and the wind blowing. There were these three huge bathtubs covered in cobwebs that I kind of climb all over. I have to laugh—my feet were really dirty. It's like I can't watch it and not notice how black they are on the soles! The whole thing looked like something out of a horror movie, like I'm the possessed girl from *The Exorcist* (how cool would it be if my head spun around?). I was completely starstruck while I was on the set. The whole time, I was thinking to myself, *OMG, that's Radley! And that's Spencer and Aria and Hanna!* Then Ian Harding, who plays Ezra, came up to me and introduced himself. He knew who I was! How crazy is that? The cast posted pics with me on their Instagrams! It was a total dream (or should I say nightmare?) come true. The best part was the *PLL* fan reaction. People started asking, "Is Maddie actually A?" and, "Is she going to be a series regular?" Don't I wish!

I feel like all the small acting roles I did and my work in videos with people like Todrick Hall (I was in "Freaks Like Me" with the *Dance Moms* cast and played Alice in Wonderland in his "Taylor in Wonderland" one) were all preparing me for the big screen. Shooting a movie is something I've always wanted to do. Making *The Book of Henry* was the best experience of my entire life. Everyone on the set—Naomi Watts, Jacob Tremblay, Jaeden Lieberher—became my family. And I learned so much from all of them, especially Naomi, who's been nominated for two Academy Awards and is an amazing actress. The first day working together she asked me where I lived. I said, "Pittsburgh, but I have an apartment right now in L.A., too."

She nodded. "Because of all the movies you do."

"Um, actually . . . this is my first."

"Are you kidding?" she asked. "I would never know. You're a natural!" Well, that made me feel better! She brought her boys, Sasha and Sammy, to the set. Her younger son, Sammy, is a tap dancer and I told him, "I saw your videos. You're good." They have a Yorkie named Bob that they would also bring to the set every day. Sam made another video where he was screaming, "Bob, I met Maddie!" So cute. I had my own little fanboy on set.

Because the movie was being shot in White Plains, New York, I had to live in Westchester in my own apartment for six weeks. My mom couldn't be there—she was stuck filming *Dance Moms* in L.A. So all she got to see was my table read and my screen test. That was the hardest part for me—being separated from her for so long. My stepfather, Greg; my publicist, Kelly Marie; and Jessica, a close family friend who lives in New York, took turns staying with me. I felt like I had three different people circling around me—one would come in, one would go out; the next one would follow. It was fine, but I really just wanted one person there: I wanted my mom. I wanted her to be there for this huge moment in my life and career, and it made me sad that she wasn't. I would call her and text her and catch her up on how things were going, but it's not the same. It was really the first time I felt like I was growing up.

I think most teens feel like I do: There's this tug-of-war that happens in your heart. You want to be on your own, to break free and become your own person, but your mother knows you better than anyone else (mine can read my mind). I don't tell her very often, but I need her. When something happens—good or bad—she's the person I want to run to. And being away from her for that many weeks kind of drove that point home for me. Just recently, we went to a screening of the film. Finally, she got to see what I had been up to.

"Oh my gosh, Maddie," she said, hugging me extra tight. "You're wonderful." She cried the whole movie (fair warning: It's a major tearjerker), and, believe it or not, so did Mackenzie. I'm so proud of this project, but also proud that it was my first time doing something totally new all by myself. It felt a little like walking on a high wire without a safety net—my mom wasn't there to catch me if I fell. Moms complain a lot about how hard it is when your kids get older and you "lose" them and have an empty nest. But it's hard for us kids, too. The good news is I'm only fourteen; I'm not ready to move out yet! And even when I do, I might just give my mom her own set of keys . . .

## *Dear Maddie*

**My longtime dance studio is closing and I have to go to a new one. I'm so sad and scared—what if the girls there hate me? What if the teachers are evil? My studio was my second home!**

It's always hard to leave a studio—the people there become your family. But just because you won't see each other every day doesn't mean they need to disappear from your life. You can stay in touch—maybe some will even go to the new place, too? As for starting at a new studio, don't assume the worst. If you do, you'll shut yourself out from good things and good people. No one likes a Debbie Downer. You have to go in thinking and believing it's going to be just as good as (maybe even better than) your old studio, and give it your best shot in the friendship department. Be warm, be friendly, be open. Give it a chance!

**Everyone who competes has to pay for these expensive costumes and my family just can't afford them. I'm embarrassed to tell my dance coach, and I'm afraid she'll kick me off the team.**

She won't kick you off! You haven't done anything

wrong; your family just isn't made of money. So what? There are some moms at my studio who do work at the front desk, help file stuff, organize the costume closet, etc. when they're struggling to pay tuition. Talk to your coach and say, "Look, I can't afford to pay for a costume right now. Can we work something out?" Be up-front early—not the week before the competition—so you can figure out a plan.

**It feels like everything I try, I fail at. Everyone has a talent but me!**

People aren't always good at something right away—sometimes it takes time and a lot of practice. When you try something and don't nail it, do you just get upset or frustrated and abandon it? I really believe that you can achieve anything if you work hard at it. There are lots of things I'm good at and lots of things I'm not good at. My older brothers tried their best to teach me a sport: basketball, soccer, hockey, you name it. I'm a klutz. I can't throw a ball. So that's just not my thing. But that doesn't mean I'm a failure—and you're not one either. You just have to keep searching for the "thing" that you love so much you want to excel in it. And when you find that passion, don't let go. Keep plugging away till it sticks.

# *Today Is a Beautiful Day to . . .*

✳ **Wear a big bow—**à la JoJo (all the time!) and Sia/me that one time on the red carpet. It was a tease to the video for "The Greatest," but those giant black bows were kinda hard to miss. Turn heads with your dramatic do! It shows you've got confidence and you don't mind standing out in a crowd.

✳ **Nominate someone to take on a challenge!** My friends just dared me to do the twenty-two-push-up challenge to raise awareness for veteran suicide—and I passed it on to three more peeps. And you better believe I did the ice bucket challenge for ALS! It was fun and it spread the word about important issues.

✳ **Hit refresh on something in your life:** Move things around your room so it's more feng shui; cook something you love to eat without cutting any corners—like marinara from scratch; fill your home with flowers (even better if they're picked from your backyard) to bring some color and scent to your space.

· Chapter Eight ·

MY STYLE FILE

When I was younger, my mom did all the shopping and styling for me—and I have the "fashion don't" pics to prove it! Yeah, sure, I was cute—but those poufy dresses, matching headbands, and Mary Janes? Eek! What I wore back then I would never wear now, but that's because I'm a teenager, and my style has evolved into something that reflects the real me: part girly-girl, part tomboy, and all about feeling comfy. I think my passion for fashion really started up a few years ago when I went to my first New York Fashion Week. *Elle* magazine and *Teen Vogue* both invited me to attend the runway shows for them, and I soaked it all in. At the Alice + Olivia show, I got to hang with *The Carrie Diaries/Soul Surfer* star AnnaSophia Robb, who told me she was a fan of *Dance Moms*. I met designers Rosie Assoulin, Karen Walker, and Gilles Mendel of J. Mendel. I got to "take over" for a day at *Seventeen* magazine recently, too, raiding the fashion closet and picking out my fave pieces to spotlight that issue. I felt like I was in *The Devil Wears Prada* (minus the mean editor—all the people who work there are so nice!).

I've walked in a few runway shows as well for Ralph Lauren. I love getting a sneak peek at what the new colors and trends will be for the next season. Sitting in the front row is amazing! Last year, I went to Rebecca Minkoff, Betsey Johnson, Opening Ceremony, Tommy Hilfiger, Zac Posen, Ralph Lauren, and Christian Siriano. Fashion Week is always a whirlwind, and I love it, but I get really nervous that a model is going to fall on the runway. One time, I was watching an Opening Ceremony fashion show, and a girl fell right in front of me . . . then another . . . then another. It took a few minutes for the audience (and me!) to figure out it was part of the show; they were falling on purpose. At the end, they all got up and broke out into a dance. But it kinda scarred me for life; I always think some poor model is going to wipe out!

If I spent my early years in need of a fashion makeover, you really can't blame me. While we were shooting *Dance Moms*, all I got to wear was dance clothes, day in, day out. So it wasn't like I had a lot of practice perfecting my style! When I was out of the studio, I just wasn't confident in my fashion choices. I was more worried "What will people think? Will they make fun of me for trying too hard?" But now, I really don't care. I wear whatever I like and I don't think about being trendy or in. My lazy-day look is typically shorts, jeans, or joggers; a tee tied at the waist or not; and sneakers or booties. You won't really find me in a cropped top unless it's with a high-waisted jean (I don't really like to show my stomach even though I know it's a big trend right now), and I stick to a gray/black/white palette. Kenzie is a lot more comfortable with color than I am. I might wear a pop of it, but never a lot unless it's for a party. I'm not someone who necessarily likes to stand out in a crowd. That's just me.

If I do have an event, then I work with my amazing stylist, Linda Medvene. I'll send her some ideas I might have, some looks I've seen and might like to try, and she'll roll in this rack of clothes and we'll go through it, try some stuff on, see what feels and looks good on me. I'm really lucky, because designers like Christian Siriano from *Project Runway* have actually custom-made outfits for me to wear out. I love his clothes—they're so unique, elegant, and pretty, but they also have a youthful edge. He knows I want to look fourteen not forty, so that's how he designs for me. Two of my fave outfits he made me were a two-piece bright yellow shorts set and a peach and pink floral-embroidered romper. The colors reminded me of a sunrise. Zac Posen and Wesley Nault have also designed for me—they're both so hip and cool, and we've always created fabulous one-of-a-kind looks together. Wesley did a blue strapless dress for me for my first *SYTYCD* show. It was icy blue lace and it had a Cinderella feel, absolutely magical.

If I have a style role model, I would say Gigi Hadid. She has the cutest casual outfits, like jeans and a blouse. She always looks comfortable but never sloppy. I'd like to have her closet, all of it, but first I probably need to grow a couple of inches to be her height. I hear she's like 5 foot 10!

This year, I got the opportunity to design my own clothing line and that's been a dream come true. I always felt like there was nothing good out there fashion-wise for tweens. Kids' clothes are either too childish or something I would never wear, and most of the time, adult clothes are either too big on me or feel too grown-up. I felt like there needed to be something in between, so girls can relate to what we want to wear instead of trying to look like something we're not. When they asked me to describe the feel of the collection, I came up with three words: *chill, comfy, cute.* I wanted it to be sporty but also feminine (because that's so me). I wanted to be able to mix and match the pieces so you could build a whole wardrobe of looks off of it. The best part was how we tested out the line—we sent out surveys through social media to get girls' opinions: I like this, I don't like that. I loved that feedback; it's like we built this line together.

I've been really involved in the whole process from the concept to the sketches to choosing the fabrics and pieces. We went into a boardroom, and they brought in tons of different fabrics and racks and racks of clothes. I went through them all, and got to say, "I like this cut and this style in this fabric and color." It was like piecing together a puzzle! The next step was creating samples, and once again, they really let me make the fashion choices. I could decide, "That shirt is really cute—but what can we do to make that plaid not so boring? Can we make it more sophisticated—like an adult shirt instead of a kid one?" Or "I love this skirt—but could we make it shorter?" We kept editing and editing down until we arrived on the first collection for Back to School. I love every single piece in it— and there're about thirty of them. I've done three different seasons now, and modeled the collection for ads and the website. I love that the colors are so me—nothing bubblegum pink or too bright, just earthy and cool—and you can actually move comfortably in the clothes. As a dance kid, that's a must. The clothes are being sold exclusively at Nordstrom and also online at MaddieStyle.com, and I'm really proud to have my name on them.

I think girls should dress the way they feel—and that can change daily. Some mornings I get up and I'm in a biker jacket mood; other days it's a comfy plaid shirt. The point is, you should always think of your style as an extension of yourself— you wear it, it doesn't wear you. You should wear what moves you—that became the tagline for my collection. This is the perfect time in your life to start piecing together your style— you can actually choose what you like, not what your mom picks out for you! But before you shop till you drop, start by combing through your closet: What's in there that already works? What can you recycle? What needs to go to Goodwill or to your little sis (you're welcome, Kenzie) because you haven't worn it/seen it in a year and you don't like it/fit into it anymore? Once you cut the closet clutter, you're ready to gather a few new pieces.

# Ten Things Every Girl Needs in Her Closet

*1* **A denim jacket.** It can be light wash or dark wash, ripped or not ripped. Basically, you can't go wrong with a jean jacket—you can wear it over anything, from a tee or a tank to a cute sundress, and it's a great layering piece. My fave hits just at the waist, but I also love the cute cropped styles out there and the vest versions.

*2* **Skinny jeans.** You can dress them up, you can dress them down. I've worn mine to a party with a sequin jacket! Dark blue or black high-waisted ones look the most "put together" (as my stylist Linda will say) when you pair them with a jacket or sweater. They just have to fit perfectly—no bagging or pinching anywhere, especially not at the knees, butt, or waist—and be the perfect length. Mine stop right below the ankle bone so I can wear them with both sneakers and heels.

*3* **Boyfriend jeans.** I have a lot of pairs of these because they're so comfy and easy to wear with anything. They can be ripped, worn, sand-washed—they should look a little lived-in. Try them on before you buy them to make sure they don't look too big or baggy—the silhouette is supposed to be slouchy but not sloppy. I like to cuff mine and roll them up mid-calf. I will literally wear anything with them—a tee, a sweatshirt, a cute cropped jacket. My mom will groan, "Not those jeans again!"

4  **A basic white and a basic black tee.** If you find some inexpensive ones, it's always a good idea to stock up (in case your little sister steals yours). I like ones that are soft with a relaxed fit, with a not-too-high round neck and not-too-plungey V-neck (I'm really picky!). I know a lot of people who spend $80 on a designer black T-shirt, but honestly those look the same as one I spent a few dollars on.

5  **Ballerina flats.** You don't have to be a dancer to own a pair of these. They're a must-have for me, and I'll wear them with anything from skirts and jeans to shorts and dresses. Black and beige are the most neutral, but there are a lot of options: I once wore gold metallic ones to the Kids' Choice Awards.

6  **A mini backpack.** I'll be honest: I don't usually carry a bag; I just grab my phone and put it in my pocket. But if I'm

traveling or have to bring snacks, water, makeup, *whatever* with me on the go, a small backpack is perfect. It leaves my hands free (to text!), and it's light and roomy. Look for colors that will go with anything, like black, brown, navy, gray, or white. And it should be made of sturdy material that won't tear, like leather, vinyl, or coated canvas.

7  **Sneakers.** Not the ones you'd wear to PE class, I'm talking a stylish pair you can wear out and about. I'm currently obsessed with my Adidas Superstars. I have the basic white, but when I did a cover shoot with *Seventeen* recently, they had every color of the rainbow and I was so excited. I wore the gray ones on the cover. I also love a basic basketball shoe (like a Chuck Taylor) in low- or high-top. Make sure whatever kicks you choose are comfy (there's nothing worse than sneakers that rub!), then make them your signature shoe.

8  **A cute clutch.** So here's the thing about these little bags—they don't hold a lot. I can usually barely fit my phone and some lip gloss in them! But when you're going out and you're dressed up, you really need one to accessorize the outfit. I have a few amazing ones by Edie Parker or Benedetta Bruzziches that look fun on the red carpet. I

think the key is to go for something that catches the eye—it can be glittery, colorful, whimsical, whatever you personally prefer. I don't like mine to be too matchy-matchy with my shoes or my outfit. It can add a pop of color or even make you smile because it's fun and different—like the beaded wristlet I carried to a *People* party that said WOW on it.

*9*   **A plaid flannel shirt.** When I don't know what to wear, I reach for one of these because it's just so easy and looks good on anyone. You can wear it open, button it up, tie it around your waist. I think it's the perfect layering piece and a way to add warmth, color, and pattern to even the most basic (or boring) outfit.

*10*   **A bomber jacket.** This is a classic that never goes out of style—my mom says she used to wear them. I kinda want one in every color this year! I like how they feel casual and tailored at the same time—I even wore one to New York Fashion Week. You can get a basic in black, olive, or brown, or go for one with different-colored sleeves (we created one for my collection with metallic sleeves—so cool). Even more fun: Add a few pins or patches to it.

## Fashion Emergencies

My friends and I are always freaking out when something happens to our clothes or shoes (because in life and in fashion, stuff happens!). Linda has this cute little emergency kit she carries with her for just those situations. She's a whiz at working things out . . .

**You get lipstick on your fave white sweater.** Take one of those little white triangular makeup sponges you find in the drugstore and wipe it *dry* across the stain. The sponge should pull the color right out. If that doesn't get it all, use a Shout stain-remover wipe to clean off the rest. They're magic.

**You rip your best pair of jeans.** Patches are so cool right now—and a great, easy fix for a tear. You can choose a smiley face, a peace sign, a word—anything that speaks to you. You can even patch with another shade of denim, then sew another patch on top of that. Look at this emergency as a blessing in disguise: You now get to creatively embellish your plain ol' jeans!

**The hem on your cute dress suddenly unravels.** Get yourself to the beauty-supply store and pick up Topstick, an inexpensive double-sided tape that comes in different widths. Toss this little yellow box in your bag for whenever you need it. In this situation, apply a piece to the underside of the hem to hold it in place till you can get home and stitch it back up.

**You accidentally toss a white tee in with a red hoodie in the laundry.** So you now have a one-of-a-kind work of art! Let everyone think you bought that pink tie-dye tee (not that you created it in the rinse cycle). It will look great with denim shorts or under a jean jacket. Wear it proud and don't cry over the unexpected dye job.

**You scuff your new leather boots.** A damp towel (not a soaking-wet one) rubbed on the spot should smooth it out. If it's not a perfect fix, you can take it to a shoemaker, who can reapply color. But the vintage look is so in right now, maybe you should embrace the lived-in look instead of trying to get it out?

**You snag your best cardigan.** Use a needle—or, if you're in a pinch at school, a pen (top on!) or paper clip—to pull the loosened thread from the outside in.

# What's Today's Fashion Mood?

The way I choose my outfit depends on a lot of things: where I'm going, the weather, what's not wrinkled or dirty (not kidding!), and what do I feel like today and how do I dress the part?

**"I'm feeling sporty."** Think pieces that have a tomboy feel—boyfriend jeans, sweats, varsity jackets/sweaters, comfy hoodies, high-top sneakers. You can go with a team tee if you have a favorite (go Pirates!) or even a cute baseball cap. Just don't overdo it—you don't want to look like you're hanging out in the boys' locker room all the time or borrowing from your brother's closet. This is kind of my everyday style because it's so comfy and easy to wear anywhere.

**"I'm feeling dramatic."** Pick fabrics that feel a little posh—like velvet, satin, suede, cashmere, and go for bold colors and sparkling accessories like gold/silver bracelets, belts, and shoes. I think this look is all about the details: beading, buttons, embroidery, metallic trim—anything that catches the eye. I'm most likely to choose this style if I'm walking a red carpet—I might pick a bright yellow two-piece shorts set (like the one I wore to the *People* Ones to Watch event) or a bold pink romper (like the one I wore to the Teen Choice Awards) and pair it with a glittery crystal clutch and high heels.

· **"I'm feeling girly."** Choose soft, flowy materials like chiffon, silk, even lace, in white or pastel colors, and look for floral prints that feel a little delicate. It should feel feminine, but not too "little girl." For example, a bowed blouse is pretty, but not when you're wearing bows on your hair and shoes, too! A skirt or dress (long or short) is always ladylike, but you can also wear shorts and white jeans. I like ballet slippers or pointy-toed shoes when I'm in this mood; also maybe some delicate jewelry like a simple pendant or stud earrings. I might also balance it out with something unexpected, like a pink mini backpack or rose-gold sunglasses.

**"I'm feeling boho."** Coachella-inspired looks can be so much fun! Try a bell-sleeved top that laces up, an off-the-shoulder blouse or romper, a crocheted sweater, ripped jeans, even a fringy skirt or vest. When I think of this style, I think earthy colors, like brown, orange, and sunflower gold. A slouchy hobo bag goes great, and so do ankle booties. I think this look is more Kalani than me (she looks so good in a floppy hat!), but if I'm feeling artsy and creative, I might give it a try!

**"I'm feeling edgy."** A leather or vegan leather moto jacket is a great investment for an edgy-girl look. I kind of channel my inner Aria from *Pretty Little Liars* and think dark details—maybe a vintage rock tee with dark-wash jeans to go with it? Details like buckles, zippers, and studding are also important; a chain-link shoulder bag works, and so do mirrored sunglasses. This look gives you a lot of confidence because you feel like a tough girl in it!

## A Few of My Favorite Bling

I never really thought I'd be a ring person, but I love the four I have. They're each very special and sentimental; I stack them or wear them on different fingers. The first is a red enamel heart ring from Jordan Askill. His brother is Sia's director, and he made it for me and gave it to me when we were shooting "Elastic Heart." Jen Meyer designed my SISTER necklace and was so flattered that I never take it off, she gave me a pair of rings to go with it. One has a tiny little diamond in it. The fourth ring is a gold open T-shaped ring I just got the other day from XIV Karats in Beverly Hills. My friend got the same one.

I also love my diamond stud earrings. They were a present from my mom for my thirteenth birthday and they are so bright and twinkly. They really do go with everything, so I just leave them in all the time.

# Five Fashion Rules You Should Break

## (FROM LINDA, MADDIE'S STYLIST)

*1 "Your bag should match your outfit."*

Just the opposite! I feel like every girl needs a hip, fun, colorful purse and it should be anything but matchy-matchy. Maddie recently wore an orange romper, and I paired it with a bright yellow clutch. The bag is what creates the wow factor that every outfit needs when you're going to a party or event. If you're not carrying a clutch, then use your shoes to add interest and a pop of color. Not matching is whimsical, youthful, and fun.

*2 "Accessorize, accessorize, accessorize!"*

My philosophy 90 percent of the time is "Less is more," especially when you're young. A fourteen-year-old girl doesn't need a huge statement necklace or armfuls of bracelets—unless you're truly feeling it (see rule #5). For Maddie, I go with small, simple, delicate jewelry—Jennifer Meyer is great, and Claire's and Target have some inexpensive options. I also think you have to be careful with how many different accessories you pile on: a hat, a scarf, pins, sunglasses, sparkly earrings. All are fun, but not at the same time. Your eye doesn't know where to look and you wind up overdone.

*3 "You're too young to be wearing heels."*
I think a sensible heel—about an inch and a half in height—is perfectly fine. It makes you look taller and walk more confidently. Save the stilettos till you're a little older!

*4 "Never mix and match patterns."*
If you're feeling it, go for it. You can make it subtle—say, by tying a plaid shirt around your waist when you're already wearing a striped sweater and jeans. Try to let one print be "in charge" and dominant, and the other can be the accent. In general, the simpler and more graphic the prints, the easier they are to pair.

*5 "You should wear what's in."*
Never wear something just because it's in a magazine or your mom or your BFF says they like it. *You* have to like it. When I put something on Maddie, I can tell right away if she's into it: Her face lights up and she struts around; her shoulders don't tense up. What it boils down to is this: If you love it and you feel it, you're gonna rock it. You should have a voice in your fashion choices; don't let anyone dictate your style for you.

## Dear Maddie

**Someone I know wrote a mean comment under a pic I posted on Instagram. They said I look bad in it, but I like the photo. Should I take it down?**

Not if *you* like it. That's the only opinion that should matter. People will say what they say. It used to bother me when people made fun of me in a photo or criticized something I posted. Now I don't bother with them. You have the power; you can delete the comment and block the person from ever seeing one of your photos again. If they don't respect you, then that's the best way to deal with it. Don't let anyone ever make you feel bad about yourself. When they hate on you, they really hate themselves, and being a cyberbully is their way of trying to make themselves feel bigger and better.

**My mom won't let me do *anything*! I'm thirteen and she still thinks I'm a baby. I can't go anywhere with my friends by ourselves because she says I'm too young. But I'm not!**

I know you just want to yell and get into a fight with her over this, but that's not going to get you very far. I think you need to win your mom over and gain her trust, and that will take time. Start small: Ask her to drive you to the mall with a friend, then agree on a time and place to meet her back. She can go to her stores and you guys go to yours—but you're under the same roof, right? Check in with texts every fifteen minutes or so. That way she knows you're okay. Here's the thing: Your mom isn't being mean. She loves you and worries about you. You may not be a baby, but you're *her* baby. She's trying to protect you. The more you prove to her that you're responsible, the more freedom she'll let you have.

**I broke my foot and my dance teacher says I have to sit out the rest of the semester (eight weeks!) and "rest it." It's so unfair—I hate my life!**

I'm not someone who likes to sit on the sidelines either—it makes me feel kinda useless and I get bored really easily. So I get what you're saying. But you also have to realize that dancing, even standing on your injured foot, could cause even more damage—permanent damage. So if your doctor and your teacher tell you to rest it, I don't think you have a choice. They're doing what's best for you. Tell yourself it's not forever. Use the time to really observe the technique that's being taught in class and take notes. Be present; don't zone out. Every dancer hurts himself/herself at some time or another, and we need to let our bodies heal. You'll be back on your feet before you know it.

# Today Is a Beautiful Day to . . .

* **Get lost.** By this I mean check out someplace you've never been—a new neighborhood in your city, a park, a trail, even a far-off destination on the internet that you think you might want to visit one day. Expand your horizons . . . literally! It always amazes me when I visit somewhere new: How did I not know this existed? How did I miss it? We've gone to some pretty amazing places with the *Dance Moms* cast, like Australia (Sia's home turf!). I got to hold a koala—how crazy is that? You could just close your eyes, point to a map, and pick a destination to learn about. If it sounds cool, promise yourself you'll get there one day. I have a "gotta go there" bucket list, and I just added Dubai because it has the tallest building in the world.

* **Declutter your closet.** If you can't find anything to wear, maybe it's because your closet isn't cooperating. I'm the organization queen: All my things are arranged according to style and color. Black tees go together, blue tees go together, white tees go together—you get the picture. Same goes for my shoes, bags, dresses— it's like a department store in there, with everything

neatly folded, stacked, or tucked in its proper place. Take just one day to get your closet in working condi- tion. Take the time to make what remains tidy—if you have the patience to fold it today, you won't have to ask your mom to iron it tomorrow.

✳ **Write something.** A letter, a poem, a lyric, an entry in your journal. Pour your heart out in prose! I really love to write because it lets me tap into my imagination and sort out my feelings. Every time my tutor asks me to write a two-page essay, it winds up being five or six pages, because when I get going, I just can't stop.

· Chapter Nine ·

# MAKEUP MAVEN

*I* saw this sign the other day: MONEY CAN'T BUY HAPPINESS... BUT IT CAN BUY MAKEUP. Um, totally! Just so you know: If I wasn't a performer, I would be a makeup artist. No question about it. I'd have my own beauty vlog, and piles more makeup from Namie's and Sephora than I already own. I'd have one of those huge train cases on wheels that I would take with me everywhere, and a belt filled with tools and brushes. Like Handy Manny—but I would be Makeup Maddie! I can't help it: I walk past a makeup counter and my palms get sweaty. It's like every day, there's some fantastic new product or palette that hits the market and I have to try it out. Or I see a makeup tutorial on YouTube and I need to get the exact same liner they used. My mom is always complaining, "Maddie, how many mascaras does one girl need?" I don't have an answer for that. And I also don't have a lot of room left to store my cosmetic collection. I have so many organizers brimming with products, sponges, brushes. I have an entire vanity just to hold all my makeup products and tools. If my house was on fire, I think I would grab my fave brushes—that's how important they are to me.

My makeup obsession started when I was much younger. I was five when I started doing my own makeup for dance recitals, and I made videos when I was seven and posted them to a channel called MaddiesHairAndMakeup (original, I know!). Even back then I could blend. I could contour and cover up and apply a winged eye with a single stroke. Makeup vloggers are my real celeb crushes (apologies to Zac Efron). Kendall got to do a video with Patrick-Starr and I was so jealous. I love him. I'm also obsessed with NikkieTutorials, Jaclyn Hill, Chloe Morello . . . I could go on and on. I think what fascinates me most about all of these people is their ability to transform faces—it's like part art, part magic. I study makeup how-tos on YouTube to learn new tips and tricks and I practice all the time. I multitask: I'll be watching Netflix and applying a full face of makeup. I think I'm pretty good, but I know there is a lot of technique involved. You can't just glue on an eyelash; it takes serious skills.

Tonya Brewer does my hair and makeup and I am in awe. The first time I worked with her was for my first appearance on *Ellen* in May 2014—Sia and I were performing "Chande-lier." I loved her instantly—not just for her talent, but for her personality. She named me "Maddie Girl" and it stuck. She even bought me a vintage jean jacket for my birthday with that name embroidered on the back! I'll look in the mirror when she's done and I love what I see—it's never too heavy, never cakey, always flawless. She'll tell me what products to use, remind me to "be good to your skin," and she always stresses the importance of cleaning your tools, so I do that every time I use them. If your skin is good, your makeup is good—period. You have to take care of it or you'll break out big-time. She's done lots of things for me beyond my Sia videos at this point: red-carpet events, photo shoots, you name it. We're buds!

## Tonya Talks

"The first thing I remember about meeting Maddie Girl was how calm and cool she was, not at all fazed by the fact that she was about to go do this huge performance on a huge TV show. She had so many questions for me! She was a fan of some of my other celeb clients and wanted to know about them and if they were nice. She loves makeup as much as I do; she wanted to know about all the products I was using on her. Once I started on her hair, she took my phone and began snapping selfies. This is something she still does, by the way: After spending a day with her, I always find the cutest pictures and videos on my phone. My Snapchat story is always all her, and my close friends feel like they know her as well as I do because they are so used to seeing her on my story. She cracks me up!"—Tonya Brewer

# How to Get "'Chandelier' Face"

**Tonya says there is a certain look to it: very natural and subtle. She's done it so many times now, I swear she could apply my Sia makeup with her eyes closed!**

✳ Start by cleansing the skin with a wipe. In our case, we might be on set for several hours, so you don't want any dirt or residue hanging on.

✳ Moisturize. This step is so important because it will determine how your foundation wears. Hydrated skin is ideal so that the foundation goes on smoothly. Don't forget your neck and décolletage.

✳ Use a damp beauty blender to apply super sheer foundation. Skin should look dewy.

✳ Bronze the edges of your face with a gel bronzer (you want a touch of color, but it has to be sheer and not obvious).

✳ I know the wig covers my forehead, but Tonya always does my brows anyway 'cause I ask her to. Just brush up and fill in any sparse spots with a color that matches your natural color. Mine is kind of blond or taupe—a lightish brown that's not too dark or heavy.

* Use a small blush brush to apply a soft glowy pink to the apples of the cheeks. Then, with a fan brush, highlight the high points of the cheeks.

* Apply a lip stain that is slightly darker than your natural lip color.

* Finish by curling lashes and adding a few coats of mascara.

* * *

I've had some amazing makeup done on me for photo shoots and I save all the pics on my phone. In one I did for *Paper* magazine, Mia Yang covered my entire eyes and eyebrows in glitter. In another shot, she "freckled" my cheeks with stars and used iridescent shadow on my lids. Then there was this one fantasy pinup girl shot with bright red lips and blue eye shadow that I just love. Photo shoots are a lot of fun for me, because I get to play with all these different looks for my face and hair. For the Betsey Johnson Capezio shoot, they put hot-pink hair extensions on me. It felt very rock 'n' roll! I've worn a green bob with bangs, and a European magazine even painted me in a mustache. It's all really high fashion, so I don't mind looking a little out there. One of my fave makeup moments on *Dance Moms* was the "Broken Dolls" number. I had to actually create a dark shadow under my chin to make it look hinged like a puppet's, huge lashes and smoky eyes, and a bright pink contour with dotted-on freckles. It was creepy-cute. For the show, I was in makeup all the time—I'm talking red lipstick and fake eyelashes for pyramid. Kinda crazy: No one really wears that much makeup in a studio. You're there to sweat and work—not model.

While I love to do all kinds of crazy makeup for fun, my everyday look is a lot more minimalist. I just put on some moisturizer, a touch of concealer where I need it (like if I have shadows under my eyes or on a few blemishes), a natural mascara, and a little lip gloss—maybe a hint of cream blush on my cheeks if I'm really pale. That's it!

## Coming Clean

**First off: What type of skin do you have? Is it dry, oily, or (like mine) somewhere in between (aka combination)?**

* For dry skin, use a mild or cream cleanser—something gentle that won't make it irritated or flaky. Tonya always warns me to watch out for products that contain stuff like color or fragrance. Teen skin can be really sensitive!

* For oily skin, look for a cleanser that controls oil or blemishes, usually containing salicylic acid or other anti-acne ingredients.

* For combination skin, you might need to use a few different products, like a gentle gel or foaming cleanser all over, followed by an anti-acne and oil treatment in the T-zone or areas that you usually break out (for me, it's my forehead and chin) and lotion on the drier parts.

* Clean your skin morning and night—that means when you get up and before you go to bed. Don't scrub too hard; just a gentle but thorough wash will do. When I

take my makeup off, first I use wipes (I really like the Avon ones), and then a cleanser like Clean & Clear Deep Action 60 Second Shower Mask. It makes my face feel like baby skin. I usually shower at night, so I cleanse in the warm, steamy shower, which is good because it opens your pores.

\* Moisturize. This is one step I will never skip, because it preps and protects your skin for any makeup application. Most of us should use a light daily moisturizer— only go with a heavy one if your skin is really dry. Girls with oily skin should look for an oil-free formula that doesn't clog pores.

\* A tinted moisturizer does double duty, giving you coverage as well as smoothing your skin. If you use one with SPF, even better. Unless you like that lobster look?

After you've cleaned and moisturized, you're ready to do my fave part: makeup!

## STOCK YOUR TOOL KIT

Not all brushes are created equal—just sayin'. I have learned that over the years. The ones you might pick up at a drugstore are not always as good, because the bristles are synthetic. These work just fine for creams and concealer, but when it comes to powder or shadow, they won't hold the pigment as well. Natural bristles are softer and fluffier—but they're also much more expensive. A good brush kit can be really pricey (like $500!), so I recommend buying just a few good brushes at first and building your collection. I'd suggest four brushes: a large powder brush, a slightly smaller blusher brush (good for blush, bronzer, and highlighter—it gives a soft, natural look), and two eye shadow brushes—one about the width of your finger for applying color across the lid, and a smaller one for smudging and blending. My other makeup must-have is a blender sponge—you know, the ones shaped like little eggs? I can't live without mine and always find a million and one uses for them when I'm doing my makeup.

# Brush Up On Your Brushes

**When you go to a cosmetics counter, there are so many different sizes and types to choose from. Here are some basics so you know what to buy.**

* **Fan brush.** It literally looks like a fan. Use it to sweep on blush or highlighter, even to clean up excess powder.

* **Foundation brush.** For blending and applying liquid or cream base to your face.

* **Kabuki brush.** You can use this short, round, and super-soft brush to apply any powder product or even blend in foundation or concealer.

* **Oval brushes.** I kind of love these, because their handle is angled and that gives you a lot of control. They come in all shapes and sizes, from big (for entire face) to narrow (for eyes and lips).

* **Contour brush.** Good for bronzer and also for "sculpting" the angled parts of your face, like cheekbones and jawline. It blends out harsh lines.

* **Concealer brush.** It's short, firm, and tapered so you can zone in and apply a dot anywhere you need it.

* **Angled eye shadow brush.** For drawing medium to thick lines on the lids with either gel or powder—great for creating a winged eye.

* **Liner brush.** This one is really narrow and pointy, for when you want to draw a very precise line with gel, liquid, or powder.

* **Eye shadow brushes.** These come in a lot of different varieties: There are ones for applying base, for applying shadow to the lids, for applying color to the brow bone, and for just plain blending and detailing. It's always nice to have an assortment, but just know you don't *need* them all. I like ones with long handles that feel like a paintbrush in my hand.

* **Brow brush.** It's angled with short bristles, so you can use it to fill in your brows with shadow wherever they look sparse. Don't confuse this one with the brow brush/comb combo that you can use to shape your brows before you apply product.

✳ **Spooly brush.** You might find one of these on the back of a liner pencil. Use it to brush brows into place and blend in any color you've applied to brows so it looks natural, not drawn on.

✳ **Lip brush.** You use this short and stiff brush for defining and filling in lips.

You'll see a lot of other brushes out there, like shaders, smudgers, blenders, definers, and large, medium, small, or flat, domed, or angled variations on all of the above. Ask a makeup artist to show you what each one does before you buy it. Literally, test it out and see if you like how it works.

# ⚥ SCHOOL-DAY FACE ⚥

Keep it simple—nothing too bright or dark. You want to look your age. I also love that this makeup routine takes no more than five minutes—in case you're running late.

1 Start with a clean face. Follow with a light moisturizer. This will prep your skin—kind of like getting the surface all smooth and ready to paint on it.

2 Dot on foundation—forehead, cheeks, nose, and chin. I use my fingers or a beauty blender, but you can also use a big foundation brush or kabuki brush to go in and smooth.

3 Apply concealer where you need it. For me, that's usually under the eyes, around my nose, and the corners of my mouth, and also on any blemishes. A concealer's job is to camouflage anything you don't want people to see, e.g., breakouts or shadows. Again, you can use your fingers, a blender sponge, or a concealer brush.

4 Brush up brows and fill in any sparse spots. I'm a brow person: I'm obsessed with Zendaya's, Gigi's, and Cara De-levingne's. I like thick, not bushy, with a nice arch.

5 Keep eyes nude or neutral. Just a hint of color will open them up and make you look more awake in the a.m. Start with an eye shadow primer—this will keep the shadow from fading. Next, sweep your color all over the lid—I like something in a soft beige with a bit of shimmer to it. You can use either a cream or powder.

6 Apply one or two coats of natural mascara. I'm loving Marc Jacobs's at the moment because it really defines and lengthens without being clumpy. The Sigma Beauty one is also great and not too expensive.

7 Apply a cream blush in a rosy shade to the apples of your cheeks. I also put a touch on my lips as a tint, then top with a clear gloss.

8 Finish with a setting spray and you're ready to start your day.

## STAGE MAKEUP

### Spotlight-worthy Smoky Eyes

If you're a dancer, you should learn to master this look—it's dramatic, but you need that when you're performing. The eyes are the key to portraying the emotion of the dance, so you want yours to be seen. They should be a little exaggerated, and makeup artists often use a ton of different shadows and liners to create a really theatrical effect. I suggest starting with just a few steps and practicing. The key is to blend after every step, so there is no telltale line between the colors. "Smoky" is deep and dark, but it's also smooth and smudgy. You can probably find a really good smoky palette that has three shadows (a light, medium, and dark) that work together. I like mine in the beige/brown/bronze family, but you can also go for silver/gray/black.

1   Start by applying primer to the eyelids—this will set your base color and prevent it from fading or smudging.

2   Your base color is a neutral. I would use a taupe/beige and apply it all over the lid. If you have a three-shadow palette, you want to use the medium shade for this step.

3   Take your lightest color—usually something with a white, pink, or pearly shimmer if it's part of a palette—and apply this highlighter to your brow bone, between the brow and the crease, and angled outward. Again, blend.

4   Now apply the darkest shadow in a C shape, starting at the outside corner of your eyes and sweeping it inward

along the upper lash line, then back up and around to halfway into the crease of your eyelid. Blend well.

5 Using a black liner pencil or angled brush with powder, apply a thick line above the upper lash line. You can wing the liner out by extending the line up and out past your eye. Don't go too long with it; just a flick, ending where your natural crease in the corner starts. Now apply a thin line of eyeliner to your bottom lash line as well and gently smudge it.

6 Using a blending brush, start at the outer corner of your eye and blend toward the inside corner. I kind of do this windshield-wiper thing with my brush, to make sure there are no lines.

7 Apply fake lashes (see p. 199) or a dark, volumizing mascara. You can use a lash curler as well—it depends how dramatic you want to go. Two to three coats is a good idea, and use a lash comb to get out any clumps.

## A Red Lip That Won't Quit

Red lipstick used to scare me—I was worried it would wind up all over my teeth. Then I learned the proper way to apply it so (almost) nothing you do will make it kiss off.

1 Start with a lip conditioner/primer—this smooths every-thing out so color will go on evenly. If the lips are properly hydrated, lip products will glide on like butter. Tonya says to apply it while you do the rest of your face, then blot off any excess with a tissue.

2 Using a freshly sharpened red lip pencil and starting at the cupid's bow, line from the center to the outer corner and repeat on the opposite side.

3 Now do the bottom lip starting from the outer corner; then stop at the center and repeat on the other side.

4 Once the lips are lined, take the lipstick shade and load the product up onto a flat synthetic lip brush. Apply the lipstick in the same pattern as the pencil.

5 Once the lip is applied, step back and look at it to make sure everything is even. If not, you can make necessary adjustments and clean up the edges using a little con-cealer with a flat synthetic concealer brush.

6 Another trick: If the lipstick you're using is too shiny, you can make it matte by lightly dusting a little translucent powder on it.

## Fake Lashes That Look Real (and Stay Put)

Okay, so the first time I did this, the lashes just peeled right off and I couldn't figure out what I was doing wrong. Then I experimented, especially with the length and thickness of the lashes and the glue. Here's what I came up with.

1 Start by trimming the lashes so they don't extend beyond your own. Hold them up to your own lashes and measure. This is key! They have to be the right fit or they will not be anchored. Use small scissors to trim off the excess.

2 Dot a thin layer of adhesive to the outer edge of the fake lash, but don't stick it to your own lash line right away. Give it about fifteen to thirty seconds for the glue to get a little "tacky." This makes all the difference, I promise!

3 Now look down, and place the fake lash against your own lash line. Press the center down first, then the inner and outer corners. I open my eye, then "pinch" the lash into place. I count to ten and hold it.

# ✂ HAIR FLAIR: ONSTAGE AND IN THE STUDIO ✂

## The Basic Bun

A dancer's BFF! I've done so many over the years, I don't need a mirror to do mine anymore; I can get it smooth and tight with my eyes closed!

1  Start by brushing your hair so it's free of any knots or tangles. Now use the brush to pull hair back into a ponytail, holding it with one hand while you brush with the other. Make sure the pony is centered. I think the best height is right at the crown, but some people prefer a low bun (at the nape) or a high one (on top of the head). I use a teasing brush to smooth it, concentrating first on the top and sides, then tackling the back. The back around the nape can get tricky because of bumps. Make sure you smooth every hair flat.

2  Fasten with a hair elastic. Make sure it's tight, even if it hurts a little. You can always loosen it up, but you'll have to start all over again if it's not tight enough.

3  Use a firm-hold hair spray to get every little wisp under control, smoothing with your hand and your teasing

brush. Make sure you check the sides around your ears and the hairs at the back of your neck.

4   Now take the ponytail in your hand and twist it counter-clockwise into a tight "rope." Some dancers like to split the ponytail into two sections to make twisting easier. It really depends on how thick your hair is. I like to do it all in one.

5   Begin wrapping your "rope" around the elastic, flattening it out a little as you go around and using pins to secure. The U-shaped "digger" hair pins are key. I use a ton; I would honestly recommend a minimum of twenty. Any fewer and you risk it falling out. Continue pinning till you reach the very end of your "rope," then tuck the ends under. It should kind of look like a cinnamon bun. Pin some more! Some ballerinas like to use a hairnet, but I don't. They remind me of a lunch lady! If you make your twist tight enough, you won't need the net.

6   Finish with a heavy-duty hair spray—I like Big Sexy Hair. You want to freeze your bun in place—especially if you're in a competition. If you take away two tips from this how-to, they should be "lots of pins; heavy spray!"

## The French Twist

Kenzie is constantly asking me to do this for her—she says she can't do it on herself. But it's so easy, and it always looks elegant.

1  First tip: it's actually harder to do a French twist on hair that's clean—it slips out. Bed head is better. But make sure to brush out any knots before you start (Kenzie hates that part).

2  Using a teasing brush, smooth all your hair straight back. I like to take some hair spray to make sure there are no flyaways, but you can also use spray gel. Gather your hair into a ponytail about an inch above the nape of the neck. Use your left hand to hold the pony tight, as you use your right hand to begin twisting hair in a clockwise direction, pulling it up at the same time. Make sure you twist the "rope" tightly. When you reach the end, there will be a few ends sticking out. You can leave them this way (in a "fan"), or tuck and pin them under. This is the more classic style; the other has a bit more edge.

3  Hold the "rope" by the ends with one hand while you use the other to roll the rope into your head. Now pin, pin, pin all along the rope, securing it. I'm not kidding: You

cannot use enough pins on this style. I will go through fifty.

4 When you're done pinning, spray the entire head with a firm-hold hair spray. You can add a pretty, glittery hair clip if you want. Now you're ready to dance!

## ⚞ HAIR FLAIR: GOING OUT ⚟

### Fishtail Braid

I do this style whenever my mom yells, "Maddie, hurry up!" and my hair is either wet or not cooperating. It looks complicated, but it's really not—especially when you get the hang of it.

1 Brush hair to get rid of any knots or tangles. Using a teasing brush, smooth hair back into a ponytail either at the nape of the neck or to one side, just below the ear.

2 Divide hair into two equal sections, left and right. Hold the right section with your right hand. Use your other hand to take a thin section of hair from the outside of the left section and cross it over to the inside of the right section. Transfer it to your other hand and you have two sections again. Pull the braid tight.

3   Now you're going to do the same thing with the other section. Use your left hand to hold the left section, and your other hand to take a thin strand from the outer right section and cross it over to the inside of the left section. Transfer the hair again, and you're back to two sections. Pull tight.

4   That's all there is to it! Continue picking up thin sections and repeating this pattern. When you reach the ends, secure the braid with an elastic. You're good to go.

## Polished Pony

I've worn this look on the red carpet for the Kids' Choice Awards—it's really easy. If you can make a basic pony, you've got this.

1   Brush hair to get rid of any knots or tangles. Using a teasing brush, smooth hair into a ponytail. You can decide where you want to place it: low, high, or to the side just below the ear, like I did. Make your pony, but leave a small (one-inch) section under it loose. Use an elastic to fasten your pony. It should be fairly tight, and you want to make sure there are no bumps or bulges or wispies hanging out. Use hair spray to keep things neat and tidy.

2   Now braid the loose section and secure the end of the braid with a small, clear elastic.

3   Wind the braid loosely around the base of the pony. If your hair is long, you can wind it several times. The idea is to completely cover the elastic. Tuck the ends under the elastic to secure. You can use a curling iron to give the ponytail some wave—or not! Now spray away again and you're red-carpet ready.

*Dear Maddie*

**My mom refuses to let me wear makeup to school! I'm twelve, and I think it's so unfair! My friends say I should just keep it in my locker, wear what I want, and wash it off before I get home.**

I don't think it's a good idea to go behind your mom's back and lie about it. Honesty is always the best policy when it comes to your parent. Can you sit her down and come up with a compromise? Maybe, "I'll just wear a little light mascara and some lip gloss—it will barely be noticeable?" Makeup is fun, but to be honest, I don't wear a lot of it unless I'm on a stage. Maybe your mom would allow you to wear makeup for more special occasions? Also, ask yourself why you want to wear makeup so badly: Is it because it makes you feel pretty and confident (a good argument to make with your mom) or because all your friends are doing it (not a good argument to make with your mom)?

**A new girl started in our school and I was the first person to be her friend. But as soon as the popular crowd started paying attention to her, she blew me off.**

**It's like she's found "better" friends and dumped me. I feel used!**

What you did was a really nice thing—you made a new girl who didn't have any friends feel welcome and showed her around. You were a kind and caring person. I'm sorry she's not being nice in return, but she's also shown you that she's not a reliable friend. So maybe she did you a favor: Do you really want someone around you who says she's your friend but doesn't act like it? If you really want to continue this friendship, you could talk to her and tell her how you feel. But if she's only interested in popularity, not in people, maybe it's not worth your time and effort.

**My dance costume for my contemporary solo is the ugliest thing I have ever seen! It's neon green with a huge ruffle around my butt—I look like a frog! Why is my dance teacher trying to humiliate me? What if everyone cracks up when I come out on stage?**

I have worn so many silly, weird, bizarre, ridiculous costumes for dance competitions! And at the time, I was probably just as embarrassed as you are, but now I look back on it and laugh. It didn't change my performance if I was dressed like a zombie, a cancan dancer, or even an

'80s Madonna wannabe. In fact, I've won in some of the craziest costumes with ruffles or pom-poms attached in awkward places. In "Stomp the Yard," Kenzie had to wear a bright orange wig (that was pretty funny, but don't tell her I said so). Don't dwell on what you're wearing; focus on the amazing, beautiful dancing you're going to be doing— entertain the audience. Nobody will laugh when they see how talented you are. They'll be impressed! And I don't think your teacher is trying to embarrass you on purpose. Maybe she thinks the "frog princess" look is pretty, or it really captures the essence of your choreography? Or maybe she's just color-blind? Whatever the reason, you can get through this if you let your inner beauty and confidence outshine your wardrobe.

## *Today Is a Beautiful Day to . . .*

**Be grateful.** Most of us don't usually think of what we're thankful for unless it's Thanksgiving and someone is passing the turkey and stuffing. Today, make yourself a list—a long list—of all the wonderful things and people in your life. Then, when you're feeling down in the future, take it out and remind yourself how good you've got it. My mom always says, "You don't know what you've got till it's gone." Don't wait for that time; appreciate what you have right now. And be generous with your heart, your time, and your resources. Every year, me, my mom, and Kenzie buy gifts for this amazing organization, Baby2Baby (baby2baby .org). They provide low-income children from birth to twelve years with diapers, clothing, and all the basic necessities that every child deserves. So we went to Toys "R" Us to help them stock up on toys and goodies to give the kids for Christmas. We went with our friends Jane and Lilia and filled up six carts—190 gifts total. If we had more room in our cars we probably would have gotten even more. We've made it a holiday tradition, and we love not just buying the toys but actually going and handing them out. There is nothing like a little kid's face lighting up when they tear open a present. It reminds me what Christmas is all about.

**Personalize your popcorn!** Make family movie night extra fun and flavorful with some cool toppings for your kernels.

* **Cheesy pop:** Toss 15 cups hot popcorn with 1 cup shredded cheddar, and $\frac{1}{2}$ cup each grated parmesan and grated pecorino. Spread on baking sheets and bake at 350 degrees until the cheddar melts (about three minutes). Season with salt.

* **Nutty pop:** Heat 1 cup honey and $\frac{3}{4}$ cup sugar over medium heat, stirring until the sugar dissolves, about five minutes. Stir in 1 cup peanut butter and 1 teaspoon vanilla extract. Pour over 15 cups hot popcorn and toss in 1 cup peanuts.

* **Cookies-and-cream pop:** Combine 10 ounces of white chocolate and 2 tablespoons coconut oil in a small saucepan and melt over low heat, stirring constantly. Drizzle the melted chocolate over popcorn, then top with 12 crushed Oreos.

*Chapter Ten*

# THE ME I'VE YET TO MEET

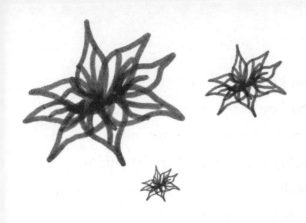

It would be a lot of fun to have a crystal ball that would let me look into the future and see what's in store. I'm not a huge fan of surprises; I'd rather know what's coming down the road so I can make plans and be prepared—that's just me. My mom says I like to have my ducks in a row. But I know you can't always know what direction your life will take you in. If you asked me three years ago, I never would have predicted I'd be touring the country with Sia, judging *SYTYCD*, or launching a clothing line. I wouldn't have done anything differently—it's all been an amazing journey so far—and I'm really grateful for every moment, even the tough or frustrating ones. They've all gotten me to where I am now, and I love my life. But as for the road ahead, it would be nice to have a hint or two. Maybe a sneak peek of what my home or husband will look like? A glimpse at how my career will evolve? I have some ideas, though . . .

Five years from now, I know I will be living in L.A. full-time. I see myself in a big apartment, with an extra bedroom in case Kenzie or some friends want to visit, a fabulous kitchen (not that I cook, but it's a nice idea!), and lots and lots of closets. A pool would also be nice so I can chill on a lounge chair and soak up the sun. I'll be driving by then, probably a cute SUV so I can roll the top down and cruise through Hollywood. But I'd really like to live close to some great shopping and restaurants so we can kind of walk over whenever the urge hits. I might have a boyfriend then, and a real acting career. I see myself reading lots of scripts and being really smart and choosy about the roles I take on—only things that really speak to me and challenge me as an actress. I know I'll also be doing more and more with Sia—concerts, videos, movies. We're a permanent part of each other's lives. I think I'll have a dog of my own because Kenzie would never part with Maliboo.

By then, Kenzie will be a huge pop star, playing to sold-out crowds at the Staples Center, and I better get free tickets, and I don't mean in the nosebleeds. I could also see her as a Nickelodeon star. Either way, she better not forget her big sis.

Ten years from now, I'll be twenty-four, so I'd like to have a real home on the West Coast—a house with a garden, a pool, a backyard, maybe a screening room and dance studio built right into it. I'm pretty practical: I know a dancer's career is very short-lived. Your body just can't take it forever. So when dance stops being something I can or want to do every day, I'll have my acting, but I also might choreograph, like Travis Wall does—maybe even a routine or two for *SYTYCD*. But I honestly think movies will be my main thing—I just feel myself being pulled in that direction. I expect to be starring in a feature film that will win me an Oscar. I'll also be filming a horror movie: I won't play the victim or kill anyone, but I'll scream my head off and be the character who escapes the creepy guy with the clown mask and buzz saw. Kenzie won't be at that premiere; she hates horror movies.

I'd love to work with the two Jennifers—Aniston and Lawrence—and Anne Hathaway. What I love about all of them is that they constantly push their boundaries when it comes to their careers. They do it all: drama, action, comedy—even, in Anne's case, musicals. I want to be an actress who's that versatile and fearless—someone who keeps you guessing what her next project will be.

I want to also be someone who gives back in a big way. Angelina Jolie is someone who really inspires me. She's so smart and generous and a voice for awareness and positive change. She's a great humanitarian, and that's something I'd like people to recognize me for as well. I'd like to travel the world, not just to see the beautiful, exciting places, but also to see how other people live and how we can help and what needs fixing. I could see myself working with an organization like UNICEF, working to help people build houses and schools, and to provide food and clean water. I want to continue to work hard to raise money to find a cure for cancer, and I have a feeling that we will see that happen in my lifetime.

I think about college, but I'm not sure if or when I would go. You never know; I might take a few years off, then decide it's time. Zac Efron was all ready to go to college—then he got the role in *17 Again*, so I guess, like him, I'd have to play it by ear and see what comes along. I do know that I will always be someone who loves reading, writing, and learning. Whether I'm in a classroom or not, that's not going to change. I'm really curious, and I like to know how and why things work. I'm a thinker, and that's never gonna change. By thirty, I see myself penning several best-sellers and a book series that's made into its own hit TV show—like *Gossip Girl*!

Broadway used to be a goal for me, but now, not so much. I also used to think it would be really fun to be a Rockette, too. I think those were little-girl goals and dreams. The ones I have for myself now are based more on reality—the directions I've been going in, and what excites me. I used to want to live in New York City, but now I'm an L.A. girl all the way. I love the weather, the energy, the creativity out here. I see myself in the center of all that, being creative and brave in my choices, a lot like Sia is. I'd love to have a clothing line that's the hit of New York Fashion Week and a makeup brand that every woman wants to wear.

If you ask me to look twenty or thirty years down the road, I'm a mom with kids doing what my mom did for me—supporting their dreams, believing in them with all my heart, and telling them to never stop being who they are, because that's what makes them so special. At this point, my mom loves being a granny (she spoils my three kids rotten), but she still dyes her hair and looks like she's a teenager. Auntie Kenzie is a lot of fun, and they beg to sleep over and hang with her. I see a few acting awards on my shelf—maybe an Emmy or an Oscar, and definitely a star on the Walk of Fame, a *Vanity Fair* or *Vogue* cover before I'm fifty . . .

A girl can dream, can't she?

# Acknowledgments

W riting a book is a lot different than doing a solo. But just like any performance, I couldn't have done it without so much help from so many people.

First, thank you to Sharon Jackson, Mel Berger, Jenni Levine, Erin O'Brien, Joe Izzi, Danielle Shebby, and everyone at WME for believing that a fourteen-year-old had enough to say to fill a book and for everything you've done to help me pursue so many of my dreams.

Natasha Simons, thank you for being such an awesome editor and making this book so great! I loved working on it with you every step of the way. Thank you as well to Jen Bergstrom, Jen Long, Jen Robinson, Stephanie DeLuca, and everyone at Gallery Books and Simon & Schuster for all their help and hard work.

Thank you to Sheryl Berk for helping me put my thoughts

together so clearly, while never telling me what to say. Without you, I would have a great diary but not a book.

To all my friends, thank you for always supporting me and being there for me. I love you guys so so so much.

To the ALDC, Lifetime, and Collins Avenue, thank you for giving me the opportunity to do what I love in front of so many people. I know I would never have had so many of the opportunities I have today if *Dance Moms* had never happened.

Kelly-Marie Smith, thank you for always being there for me and always making me laugh.

Rachel Rothman, you believed in me from the start and I can't thank you enough for all your help, encouragement, advice, and support. You are just the best!

Thank you to Scott Whitehead, and everyone at McKuin Frankel Whitehead, for all your wise legal advice and attention to detail.

Jane, you're like my second mom. I love being with you and Jack and Lilia. You make L.A. feel like home. I love you.

Sia, you've helped show me how to be the person I want to be, not the person everyone else wants me to be. I think there is no greater gift than that. Thank you, I love you.

Kenzie, I love you so much. You are the best little sister. You have so much talent and so much love and I feel really lucky to have you by my side.

Gregga, you teach me, you drive me, you put up with all of us. I love you, you make us a family.

Mom, there is no one person in the world who knows me, loves me, or supports me like you. I don't know how I got so lucky to have you as my mom but I'm so glad I did. Thank you for everything you do because you do so much. I love you so much.

And finally, to everyone who has ever watched me, come out to meet me, supported me, or paid to buy this book, thank you for helping me continue to do what I love so much. I am so grateful to get to share my thoughts and my feelings. I hope it helps inspire someone, teach someone, or make someone feel a little more understood, because even though I'm just a teenager, I promise I'm really a lot like you, too. So thank you. I love you.

# Photo Credits

© Abby Lee Dance Company: Insert 1, pgs. 3 (middle), 5, 6, 7, 10

© Glenn Nutley: Insert 2, pg. 1

All other photos courtesy of the author.